MW01147298

THE
HEART OF
US

USA TODAY BESTSELLING AUTHOR
KENNEDY FOX

The Heart of Us
Love in Isolation, #4

Special Cover Edition
Cover design: Lori Jackson Designs
Copy Editor: Editing 4 Indies

SENSITIVE MATERIAL WARNING

This book contains some **sensitive material** that we wanted to point out before you start reading. If that's something you don't want to know about, please skip this page.

This book talks about pregnancy loss and miscarriages, as well as mental, emotional, and physical abuse from a previous lover. Though these scenes don't go into great detail, it's important for us to let you know.

LOVE IN ISOLATION
SERIES READING ORDER

The Two of Us
Elijah & Cameron
A brother's best friend, opposites attract,
forced proximity romance

The Best of Us
Ryan & Kendall
A best friend's brother, opposites attract,
snowed-in together romance

The End of Us
Tristan & Piper
A bodyguard, age gap,
forced proximity romance

The Heart of Us
Easton & Tatum
An older woman/younger man age gap,
close proximity romance

The Fall of Us
Finn & Oakley
An enemies to lovers,
close proximity romance

The Joy of Us
Jase & Fallon
A close proximity romance

I'm tired of sleeping on us
I'm over dodging this crush
I'm sick of waiting ten minutes just to text you back
So you don't get to thinkin' that I'm too attached
I'm more than benefit friends
I'm more than just a weekend binge

All I'm tryna say is
And I wanna be the difference

"The Difference"
-Devin Dawson

PLAYLIST

In It Together } Joshua Howard, Marielle Kraft

Things I Can't Say | Spencer Cole, Julia Cole

Fight Song | Rachel Platten

Other Girl | Filmore

Here | Mitchell Tenpenny

Never Have I Ever | Danielle Bradbery

Some Girl | Andy Grammer

The Difference | Devin Dawson

Surrender | Natalie Taylor

Just the Way | Parmalee

CHAPTER ONE

EASTON

As HOT WATER streams down my back, I grip my shaft and pump it with visions of Tatum. Her long chestnut-brown hair, ocean-blue eyes, and full curves consume my mind.

Like every morning for the past two months, I start my day with inappropriate thoughts. Not only does Tatum work for me at my surf and swimsuit shop but she also rents the place across the hall.

A double temptation.

When I first interviewed Tatum, I felt an immediate attraction, but I kept my thoughts to myself. Not only would it be unprofessional but I could also tell she was going through something just by the vague details of her life.

She moved into the furnished apartment above my shop with two small bags. Being the nosy bastard I am, I searched her name on social media but found nothing. Not even a Facebook profile or Spotify account.

Tatum has no digital fingerprint.

Yet I didn't care because something made me want to help and protect her. That may or may not come back to bite me in the ass someday, but for now, I'm using every opportunity to get to know her better.

Aside from the mysterious aspects regarding her past, she's quiet and keeps to herself. A complete one-eighty from the last person who lived across from me.

But Tatum....she's exactly what wet dreams are made of.

The tightness in my balls overpowers me as the buildup shoots down my spine. I press a palm to the shower wall and brace myself. With my eyes closed, I picture Tatum in the bikini she tried on last week at work.

My fucking knees nearly buckled when she walked out. Even Nova, another one of my employees, was speechless.

I know Tatum's older and probably sees me as a goofy surfer boy, but the things I'd do to her—if she'd allow it—would send me straight to hell.

I'm seconds away from exploding when a screeching sound distracts me. My eyes pop open as I realize it's the smoke detector.

"You've got to be fucking kidding me," I hiss, then turn off the water. My cock is still hard and aching for release, but I wrap a towel around my waist and walk to my bedroom. Every alarm in my apartment is screaming in protest.

I take out the battery and try to reset it. The high-pitched beeping continues.

Next, I go to the living room and do the same.

The motherfuckers still blare.

The sound of the hamster wheel turning steals my attention. I look at the cage near the bookshelf, and George stares at me as he runs.

"Don't give me the stink eye. I'm trying."

I go to the kitchen and know I've found the one that's making me go deaf. Grabbing a chair, I step onto it, and seconds later, my door whips open.

There stands a frazzled Tatum in her tight pajama shorts and tank top. Her nipples are hard and standing at full attention.

Another image burned into my brain.

"What in the—?"

Her lips freeze as she looks up at me through her lashes and lands on my bare, wet torso.

I reach up and twist the cover from the detector, then pull out the battery.

"Oh...that's what took you so long." She swallows hard as her eyes linger on the towel.

"Yeah." I jump off the chair, then slide it back into place. "Shit like this would happen at the worst possible time."

Of course, I don't mention I was jerking off to images of her. I don't need to embarrass myself before nine o'clock in the morning.

"Sorry for barging in. I thought something was wrong." She crosses her arms as if she's realized she's half naked too.

I raise a brow and smirk. "You were worried about me?"

"Don't be arrogant. I was coming to rescue George."

Her words are firm, but her body language says otherwise. She's still staring at my erection poking through the fabric.

"That hamster gets more love than I do." I scowl at him but can't deny he's the cutest fur ball I've ever seen. He's become the shop's little mascot and hangs out in the office when I'm there.

Tatum smiles at George as he continues to feverishly run on his wheel. She grabs the treat bag next to the cage.

"Good morning, Sir George," she coos.

I can't hold back the grin on my face. She gave him that nickname when she first met him. Once she places the stick between the bars, he immediately takes it, then buries it underneath his bedding.

"I'll be ready in twenty," I tell her when she turns around and slides her gaze down my body again. We're working the morning shift together, but I have to unlock the door for her.

Tatum stands in silence as her eyes linger. I feel like an art model being painted for a college class. Folding my hands over my groin, I clear my throat and wait for her to snap out of her trance.

She blinks hard. "What? Sorry, I missed what you said."

I stifle a laugh and suck in my bottom lip. Tatum and I have *never* crossed the line, not even close, but right now, she's giving me all the signs that she wants to. To catch her staring at me so intensely is a rare occurrence, and I like it.

"I said I'll be ready in twenty minutes. Then we can go to the shop."

She looks down at herself. "Oh, shit. I gotta get dressed. Okay, I'll be ready in a few."

"Don't forget the coffee!" I call out as she closes the door.

"I never do," she replies, shutting it completely.

I release a long breath, uncomfortable from the blue balls I have, and decide I'll put new batteries in the smoke detectors after work. Since it's peak season, the shop's been nonstop busy. I can't complain, though, because the sales keep me afloat during the slow winter months. Summer in Florida is a hot spot filled with young college kids who want to swim, surf, and party. It was my dream to open a surf shop, and once I did, I incorporated different boards, gear, and swimwear. Since opening four years ago, it's surpassed all my financial goals and personal expectations. That doesn't mean it comes easy, though. The competition is high.

"Dressed and ready to go," I mutter when I see her waiting for me in the hall. I have George's cage in one hand and grab the tumbler from Tatum with the other.

"What's today's special flavor?" I ask, inhaling the coffee to see if I can figure it out. "Hmm...cinnamon?"

"You're getting better at this," she says as we walk toward the stairs. "Cinnamon and sprinkles."

"*Sprinkles*?"

She shrugs as we make our way to the back door of the shop. "I was in the mood for it today."

I take a sip, relishing in the cinnamon flavor and tasting the sweet sprinkles on top of the foam. "Interesting choice, but I kinda like it. Gonna turn me into one of those bougie coffee drinkers in no time."

She smiles as she takes George so I can unlock the door.

"You're bougie in every other aspect of your life, so why not?"

I furrow my brows as if I'm offended because what the fuck does that even mean? "I am *not*. I work out, surf, own a business, and take care of a hamster all on my own."

Tatum snort-laughs, which lights up my entire body. Getting a smile out of her is a win for me.

"You sound like every other frat boy out there."

"Frat boy, huh? Guess I need a den mother then. You volunteering?" I waggle my brows, knowing damn well she's ignoring my flirting.

I said I've *tried* to be professional, not that I was a saint.

Tatum's nine years older than me, and it's become very obvious since I hired her that she's more mature than me too. Not just by how she acts but also by how she presents herself. Aside from being the sexiest woman I've ever laid eyes on, Tatum's personality is what draws me to her the most.

Once we're inside, I flick on a few lights and head to the office while Tatum sets up the registers. I place George's cage on the desk and turn on my computer. Though I have a social media manager, I still check our comments and messages. I like seeing what people are saying, and when I'm feeling generous, I like to give one-time discounts to get them in the store.

As soon as it hits nine o'clock, I walk to the front and unlock the doors. Tatum follows with a folding chalkboard sign and sets it on the sidewalk that's bustling with tourists.

"What do you want it to say today?" she asks with a white marker in her hand.

Though I usually have something planned, I'm feeling rebellious today. "Can I have the marker?"

Tatum hands it over. "Be my guest."

Once I'm done writing, I take a step back and read it over. "So how do you like it? We'll sell lots of swimwear today, don't ya think?" I flash a smirk, waiting for a reaction, but her expression is flat.

"Buy a suit. Get the owner's phone number for free," she reads aloud. "Hmm...yeah. I mean, I'll be sure to direct every guy to that section today. I won't let your number go to waste."

"Thanks," I deadpan at her smart-ass remark. "Exactly what I was hoping for."

"Just helping my little student out." She pats my shoulder before leading the way into the store. "First step is getting out there, ya know? I haven't seen you bring a date home since I've been here."

That gets my heart racing, and I pop a brow. "You've been watching me, huh?"

"No, no...I mean, yes, I've noticed *only* because I live across the hall. So if this is your attempt at getting a date, I'll gladly help in any way I can. It's the least I could do since you gave me this job."

She busies herself behind the counter and avoids eye contact. However, I see right through it. Tatum has a ten-foot wall around her ninety-five percent of the time, but right now, her body language screams what she won't say aloud.

I don't have a revolving door of women coming in and out of my bedroom, and she's noticed, but she also doesn't like the idea of me dating either.

Stepping forward, I rest my arms on the countertop, then inch closer. "As much as I appreciate that, I don't need help."

"Then why are you single? I thought women in their twenties would love a secure, responsible man. I half expected I'd be pulling them off you."

I snort. "While you aren't wrong, I actually don't like women my age."

She wrinkles her nose as if she just smelled rotten eggs. "Oh."

It takes me a moment to realize what that implied. "Wait, no. Not minors. I didn't mean that. I prefer *older* women, someone who isn't going to clubs every weekend and getting shit-faced."

"Ah, see, now I don't think that's your shop's demographic, so I'm not sure that sign will work. Most of your customers are under twenty-five."

"Shit, you're right. Okay, marker, please."

She hands it over, and I go back to the sign, adding a disclaimer.

Must be over the age of thirty-five to get phone number.

"Thirty-five?" She gasps when she reads it.

"Told you. I like my women older." I flash her a wink, then work on rearranging a few displays.

A few hours pass and the shop is full of customers. There have been several comments about the sign, mostly college-aged girls who have begged to be the exception.

Tatum has rolled her eyes behind their backs at least a dozen times.

When it slows down, I order us food from a local cafe, and we take turns eating in the back. Since it's just the two of us until Aubree comes in for her shift, we can't eat together.

Just as I'm responding to an email from a vendor, Tatum rushes into my office and hides behind the door. She's breathing hard and looks frightened.

I immediately stand, worried she's having a panic attack. "What's wrong? Are you okay?"

"There's a man outside coming this way. If he asks about me, I need you to lie. *Please*. Tell him you've never seen or heard of me. Say whatever you can to get him to leave."

Her chest rises and falls rapidly. I try to wrap my head around what she just said when I hear the bell from the door.

"Please," she mouths, shaking her head. "I'm not here."

I nod, then make my way to the front. A tall man in black slacks and a blue shirt looks around the store. I'd guess he's in his late thirties to early forties. As soon as he sees me, he approaches like he's on a mission.

"Are you the owner?" he abruptly asks.

"Yes, Easton Belvedere. How can I help you today?"

He grabs something out of his jacket pocket and holds it out, showing me a flier of Tatum. "I'm Detective Justin Nichols from Nebraska. I'm looking for my wife, Tatum Nichols. She's been missing for the past two months. We're very worried about her. I got a lead that she was seen in the area, so I immediately flew here."

I study the picture as I try to wrap my brain around everything he's revealed in the past ten seconds. His *wife*? The last name on the paper isn't Benson—the one she gave me—but the photo is definitely her.

"Sorry, never seen her." I stand taller, crossing my arms over my chest.

"You sure about that?" He pins me with his eyes. At first,

he acted sincere and genuinely worried, but now, he sounds like an asshole.

Tatum wouldn't ask me to lie if it wasn't crucial, so no matter what this detective—her *husband*—says, I'm not budging.

"Positive," I reply sternly.

"Another shop down the road said she's been working here," he states. "If that's the case, you could be held liable for hiding a missing person."

"Dozens of women with long hair and blue eyes come inside my store daily. It's possible they mistook her for someone else." I shrug, not intimidated by this dickhead.

"I should warn you that I have connections with the local authorities. They got a tip, and that's what brought me here."

"You're free to look at my payroll, Detective Nichols, but there's no Tatum Nichols on it. I don't know who that is. Sorry, but I can't help you."

Justin glances around, his teeth grinding hard as I keep my stance. More customers enter, so I usher him toward the door.

"If you do see her or have any information, call this number," he demands, pushing a business card to my chest. "Any hour of the day," he adds before leaving.

What a fucking prick.

I greet and help the ladies who walked in at the perfect time, and when I'm done ringing them up, I go to my office.

Tatum's in a ball on the floor.

"Jesus." I lower to my knees and brush the hair away from her face. "Are you okay?"

"Is he gone?"

"Yes. Total douche, by the way."

"I hate that my body reacts to him this way, but—"

"You don't owe me an explanation, Tatum. Unless you

want to talk about it, of course, then I'll listen. But he's your husband?" I keep my tone calm and steady.

"Soon-to-be *ex*-husband. If he ever signs the paperwork my attorney sent him. He has a God complex, and on top of being abusive, controlling, and manipulative, he doesn't like to lose. It's why I had to leave as soon as I filed for a divorce. I knew he wouldn't accept it. I could tell by his tone that he knew you were lying. I can't stay here any longer because he'll come back," she says with certainty.

"Why didn't you file a restraining order? You deserve protection, regardless of his job title. Didn't you tell someone?" I ask softly.

"That wouldn't stop him from keeping his distance. And no. I knew no one would believe me by how he flashed our marriage on social media and made me act around his friends and business partners. The bruises were always in places people couldn't see unless I was in a—"

Memories of her in that damn bikini appear again. As I scanned my eyes down her perfect body, I remember seeing a mark on her inner thigh that looked questionable. It was almost healed, but I didn't think anything of it until now.

"So you ran," I confirm, realizing that was her only option. I should find him and go put a few marks on him.

"I saved up some cash from secret side jobs and got a prepaid phone. I had no choice but to use my car since renting would leave a paper trail, but I sold it once I decided to stay here. I knew he'd put an APB out on me, so I had to get rid of it."

It's why she changed her name for payroll.

I ball my hands into fists, feeling anger boil inside me. It's something that I haven't felt in a long-ass time. When Tatum randomly showed up needing a job and place to rent, I knew

THE HEART OF US

there was a problem. I figured she'd explain when she was ready.

"Can you drive me to the Amtrak station? Maybe I can get a ticket tonight for someplace else. While he's looking for me here, I'll escape."

"If he's already searching the area, he'll have alerts set for you for all forms of transportation out of town. I don't think running is the answer, Tatum," I tell her genuinely. "You can hide in your apartment as long as you need. He'll eventually leave when he's bored."

Tears well in her eyes, and I hate that fuckface for what he's put her through. Against my better judgment, I lean in and wipe her cheek.

"Let's talk more about it over dinner tonight. That way, you're not alone, and we can develop a solid plan. You don't have to do this alone. We can go to the authorities together."

She swallows hard, blinking up at me. I can tell she's nervous, but I'll do whatever it takes to reassure her that I'll keep her safe.

"Okay," she squeaks out. "I'm sorry for lying. I didn't want you to get involved or be put in the middle of my terrible situation."

I shake my head, angered by how her husband, a man who vowed to love her, has traumatized her. Pieces of shit like him deserve to go to jail, no matter who they are.

"Don't apologize. Put me in the dead center of it. I want to help you through this, Tatum. It's the least I can do."

She flashes a faint smile, and I help her to her feet. Our eyes meet for a moment, then I walk her to the back door. I make sure no one is watching as I lead her upstairs.

"Lock your door. I'll come over at five."

CHAPTER TWO

TATUM

ONCE I ENTER my apartment and deadbolt the door, my body finally relaxes. I feel like I can breathe once again.

The moment I saw Justin, my heart dropped into my stomach, and I nearly vomited. I made a plan to leave him a couple of months ago, and though I've feared him finding me, I never anticipated how I'd react when I saw him again.

Thankfully, Easton was working with me. He's a godsend, even if I don't deserve his kindness. He's already done so much for me, starting with the day I came in and applied for a job—one he hired me for immediately, but I'd also needed a place to stay.

After driving from Nebraska to Florida, staying in cheap motels, and only eating once a day, I didn't have much money leftover. Thankfully, he made a deal with me to take the rent out of my wages, and I'd work any shift he needed.

I moved into the furnished apartment across the hall from him the following day.

However, Easton's right about me leaving. If Justin got a tip that I was here, there's no way he'd make it easy for me to escape him again. He's been in law enforcement since before we were married fifteen years ago. He climbed the ranks quickly and gained a lot of friends who wouldn't blink twice about doing him a favor.

He's also intimidating as hell, so anyone who gets in his way always finds themselves in trouble.

Needing to relax, I decide to take a bath since Easton won't be off work for a few more hours. I feel awful for leaving him to finish the shift alone, but I know he can call Aubree to come in early if it gets too busy.

As I stand naked in front of the mirror, I look at all the places I've had bruises. They're healed on the outside, but the emotional scars will last forever. Justin once treasured my body, but when I couldn't give him what he wanted—a family —I became a human punching bag.

Having kids was one of my dreams too.

Because of him, I hate how I look. I have stretch marks, breasts that are no longer perky, and an ass that's always been on the bigger side. Justin made me feel guilty for not being perfect and didn't cherish me like a husband should. I was no longer worthy in his eyes, but he wouldn't let me leave. The emotional abuse made me believe it was what I deserved.

I cover myself, unable to bear the sight of my body any longer. Once I'm dressed, I brush my hair and wash my face. Easton's seen me undone plenty of times, and he still looks at me with stars in his eyes.

If he only knew the trauma he'd have to unravel to get close. It's why I don't open up to anyone. Justin made sure I no longer had friends by controlling my every move.

"Tatum, it's Easton. Open up," his deep baritone echoes, and I shiver. He sounds more manly than I've ever heard him.

Quickly, I check the peephole, then unlock the door. He flashes his charming smile that I've always adored and holds up a bag. "Chinese food delivery."

Grinning, I step to the side and let him in. Then I realize he's holding George's cage in his other hand.

"He wanted to tag along. Hope you don't mind."

I chuckle, locking us inside. "As long as he promises to behave."

As Easton unloads the food, I grab two plates, forks, and cups. "I don't have much for drinks. Diet Coke or juice? Oh and chocolate milk."

"Oh, I love chocolate milk. Can you put ice in mine, please?"

Slowly, I turn to face him. "That's criminal."

He sighs with an eye roll as if he's heard it before. "Save your judgments. That's how I like it."

I snicker softly as I put a few cubes in both, then pour the milk on top. "I guess I should try it before I knock it."

"That's right." He clanks his glass with mine, then we both take a sip.

"Delicious, right?" he asks.

"I mean, it tastes the same. But eventually, the ice will melt and water it down."

"That's why you don't take your sweet time drinking it. It's nice and cold, the absolute best way to have it."

"You're way too easy to please, I swear. Like the female version of a basic bitch. Except instead of coffee and Ugg boots, you only need chocolate milk over ice and a surfboard."

"Damn, you know me too well," he teases. "Oh, and sweet and sour chicken. Then I'm one happy boy."

I cough out a laugh. "Geez, you *are* basic."

We carry everything to the living room since my table is too small for the both of us and leave George on the counter. Once we sit on the couch, I turn on the TV for background noise.

"Thank you for dinner, by the way," I say, piling some of the noodles onto my plate. "I'll pay you back next payday."

"No, ma'am. This was my treat. I offered, remember?" He grabs a box of chicken and dumps half of it over rice.

I pinch my lips together, pushing back the urge to insist because I won't win anyway. "Well, thank you. I can't remember the last time I ate Chinese."

"I have it at least once a week, so feel free to put in your order anytime."

"Bachelor food, why am I not surprised?" I smirk around a forkful.

He shrugs, popping a piece of chicken in his mouth. "I mean, I can cook a little and microwave a hot dog, but nothing beats takeout."

"Did you just say you *microwave* hot dogs?"

He stares at me, unblinking. "Yes."

"Gonna need to find you a cookbook."

"What's wrong with that?"

I shake my head. "Besides the fact that you're *eating* mystery meat, they tend to explode, burn, or become rubbery from being overcooked. It's better to boil them."

"That would make too many dishes."

I snort. "Such a bachelor response too."

We continue eating in silence and watch *Manifest*, a show I've been bingeing after work. If he's never seen it, he's not making it obvious because he's following along as if he's watched every episode.

"So I have to ask about your husband. How long has he been...?" He pauses, then swallows hard as if he's choosing his next words carefully. "Been a threat to you?"

"Ten years or so," I respond shamefully. "The person I fell in love with in high school wasn't the person you met today."

Regardless of when it started, I hate that I put up with Justin's abuse for as long as I did.

"Did you ever tell anyone?"

"My little sister, Oakley, hinted she knew something was wrong by how I acted on the phone, but I'd never admitted anything until the day I left. She's going to school in California, and I didn't want to give her a reason to uproot her life. Since Oakley is sixteen years younger, I've refused to subject her to my issues. I was isolated from my friends and family for so long that they basically gave up on contacting me. Justin made sure I would have no one to depend on but him."

"Why didn't you go out there? What made you come to Florida?"

"I knew he'd check there first, and I didn't want to put my sister at risk. Florida has a lot of touristy towns, so I thought it'd be easier to find a job without any skills or education. Plus, I like the heat."

He nods, scratching his fingers over his facial hair. "I've been mulling over this all afternoon, and I think you should report him. It's not too late, and fuck his *authoritative* title. I did some research, and you can file a temporary restraining order. I'd tell your attorney you saw Justin here and ask him for help too."

"If I do that, he'll know for sure I'm here."

"Yes, but if he decides to show up again, you can have him arrested for violating the terms. He could also risk losing his job. Don't let him silence you or make you feel like a prisoner at home."

Easton's heart's in the right place, but he doesn't know Justin like I do. He won't let a piece of paper get in the way of what he wants. It would only motivate him.

"And what if I can't get one? I have no proof of the abuse."

"Well, you said he didn't allow you to be around friends and family. What else did he restrict you from?"

I twirl my fork and fight back the bile that threatens to rise as I begin to list them. "I couldn't have a job or my own money, which is why I had to sneak around for six months just to save enough to leave." Though honestly, the money I managed to make didn't last long. It's why I nearly begged Easton for this job. I was down to my last twenty dollars. "He told me what I could and couldn't wear outside of the house. Dinner had to be ready by six each night, or he'd violently twist my nipple for as many minutes as it was delayed. At first, I did those things to make him happy and get his approval, but then I realized me being miserable made *him* happy."

Easton releases a growl. "Fucking sadist."

I sigh.

He doesn't know the half of it. I lost count of how many times I felt Justin growing hard while he nearly choked me to death or how he'd compare me to the prostitutes who sucked him off during his breaks. He'd record them, then force me to watch it to "learn" what he liked. At that point, I had no interest in pleasuring him, but if I didn't, there'd be consequences.

"It'll be your word against his, but you can share your story and fight. Don't let him run you out again because then he wins. Please, *stay*. I'll be worried sick not knowing where you are or if you're okay."

"He's already won," I confirm. "I lost my home, my social life, my confidence. He's taken it all."

"Then let's come up with a plan to take it all back. You don't have to do this alone, Tatum. I'm here. I want to help."

His words are the most comforting ones I've heard in a long time. Still, I wonder if staying is the safest option for me.

Or him. Justin wouldn't think twice about hurting Easton if he came between him and me.

"If I have to arm you with pepper spray, an alarm, knife, and whatever else you can use to stop him, I will."

I bellow out a laugh. "I can't hide in my apartment forever. He'll come back to the store if he really thinks I'm here. I wouldn't be surprised if he's staking out the building right now."

"Once we alert the police that you're not a missing person and there's a restraining order against him, there's nothing he can do. You need to take away his power. He won't fucking like it but too goddamn bad. I'll hire security for the front door and make sure they have his face memorized."

My emotions begin to boil over, so I stuff another forkful of food in my mouth before I release them. Easton only knows me on a surface level, and here he is, ready to fight my battles and call in backup. For the first time, I trust someone who isn't my blood.

"I can't even begin to express how thankful I am. You have no reason to help me, yet you are." I meet his eyes, sincerely grateful to have him in my corner.

"It's because you're not used to people being nice without a motive." He gives me a wink that does more to my body than I'm willing to admit.

But he's right. The only time Justin was kind to me was in public, and even then, I knew as soon as we were behind closed doors, the mask would come off. He'd scream at me because I didn't smile enough. I wasn't social enough. I was staring at another man. Whatever bullshit excuse he could come up with to justify his actions toward me.

"My only requirement is that you continue making me the good coffee. Preferably with cinnamon and sprinkles."

I wipe my cheeks of the few tears that slipped out and smile at his dopey confession. "Alright, deal."

After we clear our plates, we watch one more episode of *Manifest* before Easton calls it a night. I think he sensed I was falling asleep and didn't want to be rude by making me stay up longer. Though I appreciate his thoughtfulness, I only closed my eyes because I felt safe with him. Otherwise, I sleep with one eye open.

"Thank you again," I say as I walk him to the door, carrying George's cage and handing it to him.

"I got Aubree to cover your shift tomorrow, and Nova will work the following day. Call your lawyer when you wake up and let him know what's going on. After I open and get the admin stuff done, I'll drive you to the courthouse."

I nod. "Will do."

Easton's always supported his employees if they need anything, and for being a younger guy, he has a good head on his shoulders. He's driven, and I've always liked that about him.

"Night, Sir George," I say, wiggling my finger between the bars. "Sweet dreams."

"Did you just tell a hamster…? You know what, never mind." Easton chuckles in pure amusement. "Good night, Tatum. Text or call me if you need anything. My phone's always on."

"I will," I reassured him.

As I begin to close the door, he quickly adds, "And lock this door. Don't answer it without checking who it is first."

"Oh my God, you sound like my father now." I roll my eyes. "My doors are always deadbolted, and I never open it before looking."

"Okay. Good. Just making sure."

"Night, Easton. Hope you have sweet dreams too," I playfully add.

"Now, I just feel like you're saying that to appease me." The corner of his lips tilts up, and I resist the urge to say more.

"Bye!" I flash him a smile, then shut the door. Once I've triple-checked the lock, I turn off the kitchen lights. Next, I check my windows even though I never open them.

Once I'm positive everything is sealed tight, I get ready for bed. My head is spinning out of control, and I'm not sure I'll be able to get any sleep with everything that's on my mind.

After an hour of tossing and turning, I take a melatonin with some chocolate milk. My lips curve into a knowing grin at the thought of Easton adding ice.

Finally, my body relaxes, and sleep takes over.

I jolt up in bed as a piercing alarm rings throughout my apartment. I quickly discover it's the smoke detectors.

But this time, it's not Easton's going off. It's mine blaring. Then I smell smoke.

"Oh my God..."

I rush out of the room and flick on a couple of lights. There's heat coming from the floor.

"Easton!"

He took the batteries out of his, and I'm not sure if he replaced them before going to bed last night.

As I whip open my door, I notice the smell is stronger in the hallway. I bang on his door with my fists, shouting out his name and rattling the doorknob.

After no response, I bang harder and scream louder.

THE HEART OF US

"Easton! Get up! There's a fire!"

Is it possible he already got out? Did he leave without me? *No*. He'd never.

But either he sleeps like the literal dead or he's not inside.

I pull my shirt over my nose, the smoke making my eyes water, and I run back into my apartment to grab my phone. If his cell is on, it might get his attention.

As it rings, I slip on my shoes. If I wait up here much longer, I won't have time to escape.

The call goes to voicemail, and panic sets in further.

I have no choice but to leave.

Suddenly, my door swings open, and I blow out a sigh of relief when I see Easton with George's cage.

"Holy fuck. We gotta go!" He holds out his hand, and I don't think twice about taking it.

Easton leads me outside, and as we cross the street, the view of the building being engulfed by flames is almost too much to handle.

The shop is completely destroyed.

What's left of our apartments will be covered in ash.

Sirens blare as fire trucks speed down the street and stop in front of us. As the firefighters rush out, Easton and I watch in shocked silence.

This couldn't have been an accident.

Deep in my gut, I feel like Justin had something to do with this. There are no coincidences when it comes to my ex seeking revenge. He knew Easton was lying and probably found out I lived above the shop.

I wouldn't put much past him at this point. He was always one step ahead of me, and now is no different. Even when I dared to fight back, he always had something worse to punish me with.

Guilt hits me hard at the realization that I'm responsible for this happening. Everything Easton's worked so hard for is gone.

He's still holding my hand, and I give it a squeeze. "I'm so sorry," I lean in and whisper loud enough for him to hear over the chaos.

Easton turns and looks at me, his eyes red. "For what?"

I swallow down the knot stuck in my throat. "This is my fault."

Before he can respond, an officer comes over. "Is there anyone else in the building?"

"No, sir. Not that I'm aware of," Easton replies. "The shops next door were vacant above."

People from the surrounding streets crowd the sidewalk. "We'll need you to provide a statement later to help us piece everything together."

"No problem," Easton says.

The officer barks at the people getting too close, and other officers set up barriers to keep everyone at a distance.

"I can't believe this," Easton mutters, visibly upset, and my heart squeezes at seeing him so distraught. "Thank God you called me."

"I was scared you had left," I admit.

Easton sets George's cage down by his feet. "I would *never* do that."

"I didn't think you would, but you weren't coming to the door or answering the phone."

"I forgot to put new batteries in those damn detectors." He shakes his head. "Thanks for making sure I was out. Who knows how long I would've been in there, maybe until it was too late. You probably saved me."

I choke out a disbelieving laugh. "Do not thank me. This has my ex's name written all over it and wouldn't have happened if he weren't looking for me."

"You really think he did this? Regardless, don't you dare blame yourself."

"It's too coincidental to be just a coincidence. He shows up asking for me, and the place goes up in flames the same night? I would be *shocked* if it wasn't his doing, honestly. That's how psychotic he is."

"Well, maybe they can do some digging and subpoena the security cameras from one of the shops on the street. If it was him, he'll be seen on one of them." Easton's jaw tightens, and I hate that he's now involved in my drama. "This isn't your fault, Tatum. Don't apologize for him. *Ever.*"

His voice is stern and final, and all I can do is nod. Suddenly, a chill swarms down my body, and I inch closer to his warmth.

"What if he's here watching right now?" I ask. "Checking if I came out or not? He probably hopes this will force me to go back to him."

Easton wraps his arm around me, pulling me close to his chest. "Well, that's not gonna happen. You'll stay with me until we figure something out."

I tilt my head and wrinkle my nose. "Where? We're both homeless at the moment."

"My family has a beach house about forty-five minutes outside of town. You'll be safe there, I promise. It has security cameras and private access. In fact, maybe you should go now while you can sneak away. That way, if he's watching, it'll be easier to slip out with the crowds."

"Wait, what? You want me to go alone?" I search his face, not wanting to leave his side.

"I have to give my statement and information for insurance. The sooner they know there's a suspect, the sooner they can start looking for him. I'll schedule an Uber and give you the code to get inside. You'll be safe there."

My nerves are uneasy at the thought of going into a strange house and not knowing any of the surroundings, but I trust Easton. If he says it's safe, I believe him.

"How long do you think it'll take for you to meet me there?"

"Might take a few hours or more. I'll go to the store and stock up on food and clothes for us. We're gonna need everything. Luckily, the beach house has a lot of amenities already, so we don't have to worry about basic shit. My brother and sister-in-law just remodeled it and packed it full."

"Wow, sounds nice."

He releases a soft chuckle. "Just wait."

CHAPTER THREE

EASTON

As soon as Tatum is in a car, I hand her George's cage and remind her to text me as soon as she gets there. I meet the officer back at his car, and he asks me to follow him to the station to give a full report.

Before I get behind the wheel, I look back at the building I've called home for the past four years. I've put in countless hours of sweat and work there. I know I can rebuild and get the shop open again, but that doesn't make it any easier to see it destroyed.

The flames are out, but smoke continues to billow out into the street. The crowd that watched from the sidewalks has cleared out. Soon, the sun rises over the horizon, providing a full view of the destruction.

Once I drive to the station, I meet with Officer Bradbery and fill him in on the events. I tell him every detail regarding Justin Nichols but don't mention Tatum. I'm not confirming shit just in case they're buddy-buddy since Justin claimed to have connections here.

"We'll have to submit this to a detective so he can get surveillance from the surrounding shops and check for any suspicious activity before the fire. If he finds any evidence of arson, it'll be sent to the district attorney because it'd be a criminal case at that point. But just be aware, stuff like this can drag on for a while. Until then, if you remember anything else, email it over. We'll stay in contact."

I thank him, and we shake hands. He seems genuine, but I don't know who I should and shouldn't trust, especially when it comes to Tatum's safety

My phone vibrates in my pocket, and when I look at the screen, I see a message from Tatum saying she and George made it. I blow out a relieved breath and text her back.

Easton: Good. Make yourself at home. I'm just leaving the station. Give me some food ideas and your clothes and shoe size.

While I wait for her response, I check my other messages and missed calls. It's no shock that news about the fire spread through the gossip mill faster than the fire itself.

Tatum: Umm...size large for shirts and leggings. Size 10/12 for shorts or jeans. Size 8 shoes.

Easton: So besides hot dogs, anything else you want me to avoid?

Tatum: No, I'm not that picky. I'll eat whatever.

I smile, knowing she's probably rolling her eyes about the hot dog comment. But the truth is, there's no timeline for how long we'll stay, so I want to stock up on food and anything else she needs. I don't like the idea of her being out in the open for Justin to find her again, and if he suspects I was lying, he may be looking for me too. The less often we leave the house, the better.

Easton: Okay, I'll do my best. I'll text you when I'm heading there.

Tatum: Sounds good. I decided to try out the bathtub. Whoever designed this bathroom has amazing taste. It's already stocked full of bubble baths, salts, and oils.

I knew she'd love it. I've only seen pictures, but knowing Piper, she went all out. Speaking of my sister-in-law, I'm gonna have to call my older brother and her soon. They live in New York City and had planned to visit the beach house for their anniversary in a couple of weeks. Now I get to break it to them that it might not be available.

Easton: Good, relax and enjoy yourself. Be there soon.

I drive to the nearest Walmart and fill up a cart of meats, drinks, snacks, and everything else I can think of. Since the bathroom seems to have everything already, I only grab a few toiletry items for myself, plus some hamster bedding and food for George. Then I realize on top of clothes, she probably needs underwear and bras too.

Easton: What size undergarments do you need?

I hold my breath, anticipating her response. She'll either call me a perv or tell me not to worry about it.

Tatum: Size 7 underwear. 36D bra.

And now I'm imagining her perfect round ass and perky breasts.

As soon as I look around the bra section, I'm immediately overwhelmed. Why the fuck are there so many options? Underwire. Push-up. T-shirt bra. Bralette. Sports. Strapless.

And don't get me started on the colors and lace or no lace. With padding or without.

No wonder women have so damn many.

Easton: Preference on style or color?

Tatum: Sports bra or wireless. Don't care what color.

Easton: Got it. This is confusing as hell, by the way.

Tatum: LOL, welcome to being a woman.

I grab a beige wireless bra, a black sports bra, and a red lace one.

That last one is purely for selfish reasons.

Next, I find the panties section and am amazed at the variety of those too. *Jesus fuck.*

I'm not about to embarrass myself a second time, so I grab a few different styles. Boy shorts, bikinis, and a thong—again for selfish reasons.

After I finish torturing myself, I move to the men's section and throw in boxer shorts, athletic shorts, joggers, and T-shirts. Then I realize I need swim trunks and should get Tatum a suit just in case.

Instead of asking her, I pick a bikini that I think she'd like and also a rash guard. Women's swimwear is basically my job, but hopefully, I did her justice.

I grab a couple of pairs of shoes for us both, and once the

cart is full, I check out.

After loading my entire back seat with the grocery bags, I send Tatum a message to let her know I'm on my way. About fifteen minutes into the drive, I muster the courage to call my brother.

"You're in so much trouble," Tristan says as soon as he picks up, and I hear Piper snicker. I'm sure he's talking about the skimpy bikinis I sent her a few days ago. She's been modeling for my shop's social media pages for a while now, and although Tristan says nothing too sexy, I purposely sent her my newest line that has very little fabric. I did it mostly to get a rise out of him, but it doesn't even matter now.

"Hey," I say, my voice strained as the reality of what's happened hits me. I've been trying to stay strong for Tatum so she wouldn't run, but now it's sinking in hard.

"Everything okay?"

"There's been a fire at the shop, and I don't know what I'm going to do. Everything's gone."

"What can we do?" Tristan asks at the same time Piper asks, "What do you need?"

"It's a really long story, but Tatum needs to use the beach house. She's one of my employees who was living in the apartment above the shop. Since we had to evacuate and she needed a place to hide from her abusive ex-husband, I gave her the address and code." My voice shakes just thinking about Justin's possible motives. What if he was trying to kill her in that fire?

"Hey, man, it's gonna be okay," Tristan tries to reassure me, but I'm worried as hell about losing the shop I invested everything I had into it.

"Well since I also need a place to stay until I figure something out, I'll be staying at the beach house too," I explain.

"So you're both staying there *together*?" Piper asks, and I hear the hint of amusement in her tone. I know exactly what she's implying. A couple of years ago, Tristan was her professional bodyguard, and when a stalker tried to kill her, he hid her at the beach house until her stalker could be caught. After a few weeks, she broke down Tristan's walls, and they've been together ever since. Regardless of their sixteen-year age gap and how completely opposite of one another they are, I've never seen my brother happier. Piper helped him in more ways than one.

"Yeah, I don't feel right leaving Tatum by herself. I have a feeling her ex had something to do with this."

"Why do you think that?" Tristan asks with a dark edge in his tone. He's always been a protective big brother, and I know he'd fix this in a snap if he could.

"He came here asking for her, but Tatum told me who he was, so I knew not to say anything. However, I think he figured out I was lying. It's very suspicious how the fire started, and I feel like he was sending a clear message."

"They'll investigate it," Tristan reassures me. "It'll be easy for them to figure out if it was arson or not."

"Yeah, but hopefully, they don't think I'm the one who did it." I blow out a frustrated breath. Anytime a business goes up in flames and is deemed arson, the owner is always the first suspect. "I'm sorry."

"For what?" Tristan asks.

"That I need to use the house. I know Piper's been working on the remodel for the past six months, and you guys are supposed to come here in a couple of weeks for your anniversary."

"Easton," Piper stops me before I can continue. "If you need the beach house, then please use it. We have a million other places we can go. Seriously. I'd rather you be safe and have a roof over your heads and focus on your business. Let me know if there's any way we can help because you know I'll send a whole team of contractors to fix it up in a jiffy."

"Yeah, man. Don't worry about it. If you need an extra set of hands, just call me," Tristan adds.

"I appreciate that, guys. I just feel bad about ruining your plans." I frown.

"We're more concerned about you than a vacation," Piper states.

"Thank you. Summer is the busiest season, and this is going to hurt us big time." I sigh at how much I'm going to lose not being open right now.

"It's gonna be okay," Tristan offers. "Let the fire chief do his job and then file an insurance claim if you can."

"Yeah, that's the plan."

"Keep us updated, okay?" Tristan says, and I promise him I will.

"Stay safe," Piper tells me, then we say goodbye.

For the past six months, they've been fixing up the beach house with hopes of coming back for their first wedding anniversary, and I feel like absolute shit that they probably won't be able to now. I know they said it's no big deal, but it is to me. Piper's put in tons of time and money to make it special for my family, and they should've been the first ones to use it.

Thirty minutes later, I pull into the driveway and start unloading the bags. On my fourth trip in, Tatum's eyes widen in surprise.

"Did you buy the entire store?"

"Pretty damn close. Who knows how long we'll be here, so might as well be prepared, right?"

"Just like a Boy Scout." She grins, moving George's cage to one side of the breakfast bar, where she watches him run around.

I hand her the bags with her items. "If there's anything you don't like, I can take it back. My feelings won't be hurt," I tell her.

"I'm sure whatever you got will be fine. Not really in the position to be picky." She shrugs.

"Keep that same attitude when you try my cooking. When I said I preferred takeout, I wasn't lying." I smirk, unloading deli meats, cheese, and bread.

"Thank you, Easton. Seriously. I don't know how I'll ever repay you for all of this, but just know that I'm very grateful. I'm really sorry this happened."

The look on her face is of pure guilt, and I hate that she's harboring blame for something she didn't do. Though at this point, there's nothing I can say to convince her otherwise.

"It's no problem, and this is *not* your fault. Yes, the situation sucks, but everything is replaceable. Plus, this place kicks our apartments' asses." I smirk, hoping to get a smile out of her. "Should we take the proper tour? My brother told me Piper added a game room. I've been dying to see it in person."

"I saw a hot tub on the patio too," she says as I shove more food in the pantry and new stainless steel fridge.

"God, I love my sister's expensive taste." I laugh. "She's a huge YouTube star with an even *bigger* taste for pricy shit."

"Really? I don't go online or watch YouTube, but that sounds pretty cool. So she makes videos?"

"Yeah, lots of vlogging and beauty-type tutorials. I really only watch them when I have time. However, I wouldn't be surprised if you've never heard of her since you aren't on social media. I should've suspected something when I couldn't find you anywhere on the internet."

"You searched for me?"

"Of course I did. Had to make sure the person moving

across the hall wasn't a secret Russian spy or something. Turns out, even if you were, your coffee was too good to evict."

"Do I strike you as someone who's a spy?" She arches a brow.

Purposely, I lower my eyes down her body, admiring every inch of bare skin she's showing. After her bath, she put her pajamas back on that she was wearing last night, which were nothing more than a thin layer of fabric.

"Honestly, you look like you could probably kick my ass if you wanted." Just imagining her thick thighs wrapped around my head has my dick reacting. I clear my throat. "But once I got to know you, I didn't worry about it anymore. I instantly saw how hard of a worker you were and how you were super kind to everyone you met."

Tatum's far more caring than I would expect from someone who's endured the trauma she has. I would've never guessed had I not witnessed her reaction to seeing Justin yesterday. The asshole turned my sweet and sexy employee into a scared shell of herself. If I ever get the chance to come face-to-face with him again, he won't have the opportunity to say a single word.

"Maybe I was just good at pretending. Could've still been a spy."

"Very true. Are you?"

She chuckles. "No, but I wouldn't tell you if I were." She winks. "It would be a cool job, though."

I burst out laughing. "I think we have different opinions on what I'd consider *cool*."

After the kitchen is clean and all the groceries are put away, we go from room to room, and I'm in shock from every update Piper made.

"We'll have to play some pool. You any good?" I ask.

"Not sure. I haven't played in years."

"Now that's a crime. We'll have to change that soon."

Next, I lead her upstairs. "There's one bathroom but two bedrooms. The bathroom downstairs, as you know, has the deep jet tub, but the shower is up here. You can have either room."

Tatum looks in both and decides on the one with the great ocean view. Honestly, I don't blame her. She sets her bags of clothes down on the freshly made bed. Whoever Piper hired to clean and stock the place did a fantastic job. You wouldn't even know there was a whole construction crew here just last week. I'm not sure if anything else needs to be done, but it looks finished to me. Knowing her, though, she probably has minor tweaks no one else would even notice.

"What's that?" Tatum asks when we enter the living room.

"Oh, that's a five-thousand-piece sailboat puzzle Tristan and Piper did a couple of years ago when they were stuck here for a few weeks."

She furrows her brows at my choice of words.

"Long story, I'll tell you later. Anyway, once it was done, I mod-podged it and was going to ship it to them, but then Piper decided she wanted it to stay here. So she got it professionally framed and hung it up. Makes for a cool piece now."

Next, I bring her to the game closet that's still packed full of board games we played anytime we came here.

"Wow...that's a lot." Her eyes widen in amazement.

I nod, then notice some newer games Piper must've bought.

We finish the rest of the tour, and once we make it back to the living room, I hear Tatum's stomach growl.

"Would you like a turkey and cheese sandwich or anything? I'm pretty certain I can't screw that up."

She laughs, grabbing a throw blanket and snuggling into

the sofa. "Sure, that'd be great. Thank you. I'm probably going to fall asleep soon, though."

"Me too. We've had a long fucking day."

I think about everything I need to handle as I prepare our meal. I have so much shit to do between getting reports and contacting the insurance company.

"You never told me how it went at the station," Tatum says after I hand her a plate and the bottle of water she asked for. I take the seat next to her, and the TV's volume is low enough for us to talk over it.

After I pop the tab of my beer and take a long sip, I tell her what the officer said.

"How will I get a temporary restraining order if I'm hiding out?" she asks while we eat.

"That might be something you'll want to ask your lawyer. I'll take you to the courthouse to file one if he thinks that's what you should do. I'd hope Justin wouldn't be stupid enough to try anything in public if he found you, but then again, I don't know him."

"No, he'd never do anything to jeopardize his *perfect* reputation, but that doesn't mean he wouldn't follow me or try to grab me or something. I have no idea if he's working alone or has the entire state of Florida searching for me at this point."

"Well, if Detective Bradbery knew of him, he didn't make it obvious. Didn't seem fazed in the least when I dropped his name as a suspect."

"That could go either way. Perhaps, the detective was prepared for you to name-drop him because he knows Justin's after me, or he has no idea what's going on. Regardless, I wouldn't give them my full trust just yet."

I can't blame her for reacting this way.

"Don't worry, I didn't. Do you mind me asking, how are

you paying for your lawyer?"

"Friend of a friend's husband. He's doing it pro bono. Without his help, I would've had to file myself, and though there's nothing I want from Justin regardless of being told half of everything is mine, I feel at ease asking him legal questions instead of googling them."

"That's good. I'm happy someone was able to help you."

"Do you think we'll have to stay indoors while we're here? I'd hate to neglect the beach." She gives me a little smile.

"Considering it's private access, I think venturing outside is safe. Maybe don't go alone, though. I'd feel better if we stayed together. Plus, now that Justin's a person of interest in the investigation, we could call in the threat if he shows up. It's on paper now, so we have a trail."

"I'm good with that. I've been cooped up long enough to last me a lifetime, so if I have to stay in, I will, but enjoying the water for a bit would be a nice change of scenery."

Once I put our dishes in the sink and clean up my mess, I head back to the living room and find Tatum asleep on the couch. Carefully, I lift her feet and take a seat, then place them in my lap. I pull the blanket over her, making sure she's fully covered.

I watch TV before deciding to text Tristan. I still need to call my parents, but I'll do that later so I don't wake her up.

Easton: It looks fucking amazing in here. You guys did a really good job designing everything. Thank you again for understanding. Tatum loves it too.

Tristan: Don't even sweat it. How are you holding up?

Easton: Besides feeling stressed, being here with Tatum isn't the worst thing.

Tristan: HA! Piper told me to tell you "she knew it!"

I roll my eyes because I can hear her voice in my head saying those exact words.

Easton: I need to somehow figure out all the inventory I had, but without my laptop, I can't access my Dropbox files. I'll probably have to fight with the insurance company a bit until they give me the final report on how the fire started.

Tristan: All your purchase and sales reports should be enough for them. Otherwise, if you give me your login info, I can print everything you need and mail it in.

Easton: I'll let you know once I speak to them, but thank you. I appreciate any help.

Tristan: Whatever you need, brother. Just text or call me.

Easton: Appreciate that. I'm exhausted, so I'll talk to you tomorrow.

It's only seven when I finally cave and wake Tatum so she can go to her bed. I double-check the locks and security system before making my way to my room with George's cage. I'm used to hearing him run on his wheel at night, and even though I found it annoying at first, now it's like white noise, and I need it to fall asleep.

I tell Tatum good night one last time before she closes her door, then crash before I even pull down the covers.

CHAPTER FOUR

TATUM

DAY 2

THE HOT SUN beaming through the windows wakes me, and though I'm in a different bed and place, I slept better than expected. I was tired as hell, but it took me some time to actually fall asleep. Probably because I had a nap on the couch with Easton sitting next to me. I hadn't expected to see him so close when he woke me.

I go to the bathroom and freshen up. The cabinets are stocked with everything I could need or want, which is a relief. I'm glad I didn't have to ask Easton to get me pads and tampons. It's bad enough he now knows my underwear and bra sizes. It's not that I'm a prude, but he's my boss. Though his little flirty comments don't go unnoticed, I've tried my best to keep my distance. Getting too close meant risking him finding out about my past.

Guess that's a moot concern now.

As soon as I'm back in my room, I pull out the clothes he bought. For a guy, he didn't do that bad. Mostly black leggings, black jean shorts, and T-shirts. He also grabbed a few sundresses that are lightweight and cute. The humidity is something I'm still getting used to.

I put on a pair of shorts and one of the racer tops. It's not something I'd normally wear since it's more revealing than I'm used to, but it's actually comfortable.

Just as I'm about to go downstairs, my phone vibrates, and I see Oakley's name on the screen. My sister has FaceTimed me every Friday since I left home. It's the only day of the week she doesn't have morning classes. Before then, we'd only text, but she insisted on seeing my face to make sure I was still alive.

"Hey, I was getting worried you forgot about me today."

"No way," she says around a yawn. "Just slept in a little. How are things? Still pretending you aren't crushing on your hot boss?"

Jesus. She's a blunt little shit.

"I'm too old to be *crushing* on anyone, nevertheless, my boss," I retort, rolling my eyes.

"Mm-hmm." She waggles her brows, then props the phone up while she starts a pot of coffee.

"So tell me what's been going on since we last talked. Did that guy from the cafe ask you out yet?" I ask so she'll stop making assumptions about Easton. Though I am interested to hear about the guy who runs into her every couple of days at the same coffeehouse.

"Mr. Suit and Tie? Nah. As soon as I told him I'm a painter and graduated with an art degree, he got all Mr. Uptight and Pompous. Apparently, he only dates women with half a brain so there's no chance they'll have a bigger IQ than him."

I smirk. "Your education probably scared him off."

"Yeah, but his loss, honestly. Better to find out he has small dick energy now rather than later in the bedroom."

I snort. "Always a silver lining."

She stops abruptly and squints at me. "Wait a minute. Where are you?"

Inhaling a slow breath, I back away from the camera and show her the room.

"Holy fuck, are you..." She lowers her voice to a whisper. "In a guy's bedroom? Please tell me it's—"

"No," I quickly say. "Before you freak out—"

My words are cut off by a knock on the door, and then Easton pokes his head in before I can answer. "Oh good, you're up. I'm making breakfast if..."

I swallow hard, and he finally notices my phone with my sister's wide-eyed expression.

"Oh shit, sorry. I shouldn't have barged in. If you're hungry, I'm making omelets."

"Sure, I'll be down in a bit." I flash him an easy smile, and he bows before closing the door behind him.

"I knew it!" Oakley squeals. "I fucking knew it, you little sleazy liar."

I scoff at her choice of words but am not fazed by them. "Shush. It's not what it looks like, okay? There was a fire."

"Wait, really? Where?"

"In the shop and our apartments. We barely made it out before it engulfed the entire building."

"Oh my God, Tate. When did this happen? You didn't call me!"

"Yesterday morning, and I knew we'd talk today. Plus, I was too exhausted to explain everything. I saw Justin across the street, he came in, and Easton covered for me. Then in the middle of the night, the place erupted in flames."

"That motherfucker. So where are you then?"

I tell her the rest of the story and reassure her that we're okay and safe now. Once she got over the initial shock, she went back to teasing me about being here with Easton. I first mentioned him when I settled in Florida and mistakenly told her he was an attractive younger man I'd let break my back.

She hasn't let me live it down.

"I want to see that coward asshole in an orange jumpsuit, handcuffed around his wrists and ankles, then thrown in a cell with alligators. Then after they've feasted on him, stick him in an electric chair that will burn off his skin and make his face melt down his half-dead body. In fact, I'd give my left tit to witness it," she states confidently.

"Christ, Oakley. It's going to take years of therapy to scrub that image from my mind now." I groan. She's always been an eccentric child, so I should be used to the frank shit that spews from her mouth, but sometimes, she still takes me by surprise.

"Which part? His death or my left tit?"

I scowl. "Smart-ass."

"Oh, like you haven't thought of a hundred ways you'd like to see him die. I'm just bold enough to say it aloud. In fact, it's called *manifesting*. You should try it. Manifest his crude and painful death." She gloats, pretending to sprinkle it into the air.

"I don't want him dead. I just want to be left alone," I state.

She gives me a pointed look.

"Okay, I'm gonna go now..." I linger uncomfortably, especially now that she knows Easton and I are basically stuck inside this house together. I know her thoughts are running wild and will soon come to the surface if I don't jump off this call. "I'm gonna go help Easton make breakfast before it gets too late."

"You mean help him take off his clothes and ravish you all day? Okay, fine. Just tell me the details later. I wanna know length *and* girth."

"Go take your meds for the delusions, okay?" I tease. "Love you, sis."

"Love you too. Take care of yourself." She says the same thing at the end of every one of our conversations.

"I will. Bye."

She blows me a kiss, then I end the call.

Oakley is the best thing that's ever happened to me. Though she's not my child, I basically raised her as mine. My mother remarried when I was thirteen, and two years later, she had Oakley. I was overprotective of her, but somewhere along the way, the roles reversed. It's how she figured out something was wrong with me. And although I wouldn't confirm what was happening until after I left, she had her suspicions. It's why she'd encourage me to seek help even when I tried to convince her everything was fine.

I set down my phone, and when I walk downstairs, I'm greeted by Easton cooking in front of the stove. Between the view of his T-shirt hugging his biceps and the spicy veggies I smell, my mouth is drooling.

"Hey, morning. Sorry for interrupting you earlier. If you're hungry, I'm making my infamous Mexican omelets."

"Oh, it's fine. And sure, I'll try some."

I look down at the counter and see a mixture of veggies, seasonings, and cheeses. "Are those jalapeños?"

"Yep. Do you not like them?"

I hold one up to my nose and wince. "I guess today's the day we find out."

Easton grabs a handful of crushed green olives and adds them to the pan. I give him a look, and he pops a brow. "What? Not an olive fan?"

"Uhh…with eggs? Didn't you say this was a Mexican omelet?" I ask without trying to hurt his feelings. "Maybe I should make *you* breakfast."

"You don't trust me?" he playfully asks. "Just give it a chance."

When he covers a thick layer of garlic powder on top, I know without a doubt, I won't be able to eat this.

Bless him for trying, though.

"Should I make us coffee?" I ask.

"If you can figure out that fancy-ass machine, go for it. I'm sure there are beans somewhere."

"It's an espresso machine. How hard can it be?"

Ten minutes later, I'm eating my own words.

"There's no reason this should be so difficult," I grumble when the machine screams out but still doesn't give me any coffee.

"Hate to say I told you so..." He smirks, uncovering the pan and checking on the food. It's been done for a couple of minutes now, but he's kept it warm on the stovetop.

I shoot him a glare. "Maybe I'll google it. Should have an instructions manual on there at least."

"Nah, we'll bother Piper and make her tell us. She'll be excited to meet you anyway."

"Oh...um, okay." Meeting any of Easton's family members makes me nervous.

He holds out his phone as we wait for her to pick up. Seconds later, her face appears on the screen.

"Hello, my favorite brother-in-law!"

"What's up, my baby sis? We need your help."

"What did you break?" she immediately asks, and I chuckle at her assumption.

"This is Tatum, by the way."

"Oh my gosh, it's so nice to put a face to a name! Easton talks about you so much. I feel like I already know you."

Heat covers my cheeks as Easton squirms next to me. "She's lying. Ignore her," he mumbles.

"I am not! You tell me how I know her date of birth, eye color, and address?"

My eyes widen in horror.

"Ignore her," he says sternly. "She helped me with payroll *one time*. Quit making me sound like a stalker."

"That explains two of the three," I say with my brows raised.

"Okay, I better come clean before I get him in trouble. I know your eye color *now* from just seeing you. I was only teasing," she states, but I notice the wink she gives him.

Now I don't know what to think.

"Anyway..." Easton drawls. "How do you work this contraption? We want coffee and it's spitting out water."

"Oh, you will love it! It makes literally the best brew ever. Did you find the beans?"

After Easton tells her we did and explains everything we've tried, she goes over it step by step until the smell of fresh coffee wafts in the air. Then she explains how to use the frother but suggests we use it with heavy whipping cream instead. Since we don't have that, I just poured regular creamer in mine since that's all I really need.

"Oh and if you open the drawer right underneath, you'll see a ton of different spices. Add some cinnamon to the top. You can thank me later," she gloats.

I instantly smile because I love putting that on top of mine.

"You and your bougie-ass coffee, I swear." Easton shakes his head. "But thank you, sis. Is Tristan around?"

"He's in the shower. I can bring you in there if you want?"

Apparently having no boundaries runs in the family.

"Nah, I don't need *either* of us to see him naked. Just tell him to text or call me later."

"Okay, let me know if you guys need anything! It was great to meet you, Tatum. Don't let Easton drive you crazy!" she sing-songs before he presses the end button.

"She is very bubbly in the morning," I say.

"Yeah, morning sex will do that to ya." He snorts, then notices my furrowed brows. "She's way too open with their personal lives. She can't help telling me more than I need to know."

That makes two of us who didn't need to know.

Once we have our cups of coffee, Easton serves the omelets.

"And some hot sauce to top it off..." he says like a master chef presenting his award-winning dish. The presentation looks good, but the weird variety of shit he added makes me wonder how it could possibly taste good.

"Thank you," I say.

"You're very welcome. Wanna sit at the table?" He grabs his plate, and I follow him.

"So you said before that your sister is sixteen years younger than you. Does that make you closer or more distant being that far apart in age?"

"We're as close as we can be living in separate states and all." *And all* meaning that I had to sneak around to talk to her in private. "Oakley and I FaceTime every Friday, so this morning I told her everything that happened and why we're here. She worries a lot."

"She's in California, right? What's she going to school for?"

"Yep. She just graduated last month with her Bachelors in Fine Arts. She also started a summer grad class a few weeks ago to get ahead for her master's degree. She's a super talented painter, like gets commissioned for some pretty awesome gigs, so she doesn't even need the extra education, but she's one of those people who's always loved school. Her brain is a sponge, and she can literally remember anything she learns once."

"Damn. I'd love school too if it came that easy."

"No kidding, right? She's an extrovert too, so she gets along with almost everyone."

"Maybe she'll come visit you someday, and I can meet her," he offers. "I bet she'd have fun in Florida too."

"Oh I know she would. She's a boy-crazy twenty-two-year-old."

I take my first bite, slowly chewing and getting used to the flavors. He watches me eagerly and I can tell he really wants me to like it, but damn, it's god-awful.

"You hate it, don't you?"

I nod, and he hands me a napkin, then I spit it out.

"I'm sorry, I really don't want to sound unappreciative."

"Nah, don't be." He grabs my plate and slides it next to him, stabbing it with his fork and taking a bite. "I'll eat it."

Easton gobbles it down like he has an iron stomach, and honestly, I don't know how it's not burning him from the inside out. Maybe I have a low tolerance to a lot of spices, but that hot sauce alone is still lingering on my tongue.

"I can make you a regular one with just cheese?" he offers when I stand to go to the kitchen.

"No, it's okay. I'm not as hungry as I thought. I'll just grab a granola bar and eat it with my coffee."

Since the kitchen is a mess, I clean it for Easton while he finishes eating. I rinse the dishes before putting them in the dishwasher, then wipe down the counters. By the time Easton brings the plates over, it's nearly spick-and-span.

"So I was thinking, since we're here indefinitely, I want to take advantage and catch some waves. There won't be much else to do, and as long as we stick together, we should be safe to go out."

"*We*? You seriously think I can surf?" I laugh. "I've been to the beach like...twice since I've been in Florida. And one of those times, it started raining five minutes after I got there, so I left."

"We gotta do the buddy system! If I go, you go."

I give him a side-eye, wondering if he's being serious or messing with me. "I'm a little old to be doing the *buddy system*, but I can watch from the beach."

"I promise you'd love it."

He's so confident and excited that I can't bear to disappoint him. It would be nice to enjoy the water while we're here, but the last thing I need to do is break something and be vulnerable while Justin's looking for me.

"I have little to no athletic skills," I tell him, neither agreeing nor disagreeing with his plan.

Easton chuckles, moving around me in the kitchen and brushing his hand along my lower back. The innocent gesture sends a spark of desire between my legs. I swallow down the hint of embarrassment, hoping he didn't notice.

"How long have you been surfing?" I ask, adding his plates to the dishwasher, then starting it.

He takes a bottle of water from the fridge, then heads for the living room. I follow and take a seat on the couch. Easton clicks on the TV and flips through the channels.

"Since I was a kid. Tristan actually taught me before he left for the military. Then I just fell in love with the way it amped me up for the day and knew I wanted a career around it. Besides teaching or going pro, opening a shop for surfboards and swimwear seemed like the next best option. Turns out, it was the one that changed my life. I can't imagine sitting in a cube for eight hours a day. Plus, I love being able to share my passion with other people. I nearly surfed professionally but didn't want to be constantly traveling and away from my parents."

"Wow," I say in amazement. I wasn't aware of his

background, and honestly, it's impressive. It makes me wish I had an outlet and passion that I could've pursued while growing up.

Easton finally grows bored from scrolling and hands me the remote. I eventually land on an old movie I used to binge-watch as a teenager.

"Is that Lisa Kudrow? Wow, I've never heard of this one," he exclaims a few minutes into it, and I give him a look of shock.

"Are you serious? Oh my God. The number of times I have seen this is too many to count."

"This can't be real..." he says after fifteen minutes. Romy and Michele are flashing back to when Christy Masters stuck magnets on Michele's back. The level of cringe is high, but that's what made it such a classic comedy.

"Are you not aware of corny 90s movies? Wait...were you even born then?" I tease, and he smacks me with a throw pillow.

"Age jokes, really? Okay, Grandma. Sorry I wasn't around to witness the first man land on the moon like you."

I roll my eyes and chuck the pillow back at him. "That's not even comparable."

"So besides having god-awful taste in movies, what else don't I know about you? Do you have any hobbies?"

"Um..." I chew on my lower lip, taking a moment to think about his question because I wasn't allowed to have *hobbies* outside of taking care of the house. Justin watched me like I had a warrant out for murder. "Between a lock code that recorded every time I left the house and inside and outside security cameras, I wasn't able to do much that didn't involve him plastered to my side," I admit, which even takes me by surprise. "I enjoy yoga and meditation, but truthfully, I only started a month or two ago, so I'm still learning. I guess I need to figure out what activities I do like."

"I'm really sorry to hear you had to go through that. If you hadn't told me, I would've never guessed. You're so damn strong, Tatum. Reserved and quiet, yes, but you hold your own. I've always noticed that."

"Trauma responses can cause different reactions when you're no longer in that situation. I lived in shock for the first month, surprised that I had actually gotten away from him. Looking over my shoulder happened quite often and still does. I guess I'm good at hiding it. Once I was free, I knew I was in charge of my own life again, and I wasn't going to allow him to take that from me." I shrug, then add, "Well, that's what I like to think anyway. The moment I saw him coming toward the shop, my fight response failed."

"It didn't fail," he says softly. "You removed yourself from the situation. You can't just turn off the fear he ingrained into you for years in just a few weeks. But regardless of that, you are strong. You got yourself out of an impossible situation. Managed to not only get the money but also the courage to file for a divorce and leave."

"I should've left sooner," I admit. "I knew I wanted to for years and was actually getting ready to bail shortly before the pandemic happened. Then everything changed. Instead of Justin working at the office, he worked remotely, and I was stuck with him twenty-four hours a day. Like most abuse victims, the lockdowns made it worse."

"Jesus, I hadn't even thought of that." He shakes his head as if he's trying to hold in his anger. "Well, let's make this *lockdown* version a helluva fun time. We'll erase your bad memories and replace them with only good ones."

CHAPTER FIVE

EASTON

DAY 3

FOR THE PAST TWO HOURS, I've been transferred to different departments, put on hold, then transferred again. I'm stuck in some sort of weird loop, and I'm getting nowhere fast. After the last insurance agent wasn't able to help, I was told they'd escalate my case to someone higher up. Considering the fire happened less than forty-eight hours ago, things feel as if they're permanently suspended in the air. My frustration is building, but I try to stay calm and collected because this is just the beginning. Probably doesn't help that it's Saturday and some people aren't in the office.

Nearly forty-five minutes pass when my phone buzzes from an unknown number. I usually don't answer, but considering the circumstances, this time I do.

"Hello, sir. We've been trying to contact you to extend your car warranty. Are you avail—?"

I end the call and release a groan just as Tatum comes downstairs.

"Everything okay?" she asks.

"No. I can't get calls back, and I'm annoyed."

She sucks in a deep breath. "I'm sorry."

"Not your fault," I remind her, then realize she's wearing leggings and a tank top. "Going somewhere?"

She throws a towel over her shoulder and grins. "I was thinking about heading outside for a meditation session. I think some fresh air and sunshine will do me good."

I nod just as my phone buzzes. "Okay, but don't go too far. Have fun," I tell her with a wink.

"What about all this buddy system stuff?" she asks with a brow popped.

"I won't take my eyes off you, Tatum," I promise, and I think I see a hint of blush cover her cheeks.

Her mouth opens just as I get another call. Right now, I wish we could continue this conversation, but she grins and sashays outside.

"Mr. Belvedere. This is Sabrina Kellington, from the insurance company. Sorry, I've been swamped and just got the notification that you needed to speak with me. Just wanted to fill you in with what's going on so far. Since it's the weekend, people are hard to reach. Didn't want to call you with no information, so I've been on the phone all morning," she tells me.

"I appreciate that," I say. I can hear the clicks of her fingers on the keyboard.

"So I'm sending an appraiser out first thing Monday morning. He is scheduled to show up around eight and take photographs of the damage. Right now, it seems like I'll need proof of your current inventory. Do you happen to have that information readily available that you can send over?"

"Not *readily* available. All of my files were stored on my computer in my office."

"I understand. The sooner you can get a full list together, the better. That way, we can file the claim for review."

"No problem. Do you know what the timeline is for all of this? Like how long it will take to get things cleaned up, rebuilt, and replaced?" I stare out the windows at Tatum, a gorgeous sight to see.

"Unfortunately, not yet. Once all the information is submitted, it goes through an appraiser, then an approval process before we can send a check. After that, it depends on the contractor's timelines. It can take anywhere from two to six months and sometimes longer, depending on the amount of damage. And sometimes, it's a complete loss, which means you'll have to build from scratch. But I'll know more once the appraiser submits everything. We're already in contact with your mortgage company."

I let out a breath and focus on where Tatum's sitting cross-legged at the edge of the property facing the ocean. The sun reflects off her hair, and she's been in that position since I started this call. The focus she has to sit on that towel without moving is incredible.

"That makes sense."

The agent promises she won't let anything fall to the wayside and will work diligently to make sure the process moves quickly.

"I appreciate that," I say.

She gives me her email address and the number to her direct line.

"I'll try to get everything to you by early next week," I tell her.

"That'd be great. The sooner, the better," she states before the call ends.

Now I'm more stressed than I was before. Without my computer, it's going to get complicated to get all of that information. I'll probably need to call Tristan to help get me out of another bind, something I hate doing.

I grab a bottle of water, and when I round the corner, Tatum enters.

"Get it all sorted?" She's wearing a smile, and I can't help but notice how relaxed she seems after her meditation session.

"Not really. Mostly an impossible to-do list," I admit.

"One thing at a time," she calmly states, and it makes me wonder how many times she's repeated that to herself.

Before I can say anything, the doorbell rings. Tatum jumps at the sound, then laughs at herself. It's not lost on me how jumpy she is even in this safe space. Noticing it's a delivery person, I open the door and sign for the heavy box. I bring it to the breakfast bar, then grab a pair of scissors.

"Did you order something?" I ask, and Tatum shakes her head.

"Weird." I cut through the tape and find a note at the top. I glance over the first few lines, then read it aloud.

Easton,

The iPad is for Tatum to keep her occupied while you two are together. Hopefully, it will help keep her busy because I've been there and about lost my mind without connection to the outside world. The MacBook Pro is for you since I know you'll have a lot of stuff to take care of, and we love a busy boss boy. I'm really sorry all of this happened to you. If you need anything, don't be a stubborn Belvedere, and just ask. We're always here for you.

Love your favorite sister EVER and that one guy you're forced to love,
Piper and Tristan
(For the record, I told her not to call you a boss boy.)

I snort-laugh and hand the iPad box toward Tatum. She doesn't take it from me. "No, I can't accept it. It's too much. I'll never be able to repay her."

I can see her hesitation and try to soften my voice as I speak. "Piper is *very* extra and she loves to give people gifts. It's her love language. Plus, you deserve it. Not gonna make you, but she did get you the Pro one." I flash her a wink.

A smile eventually spreads across her face, and she takes the box. "I've never had anything as expensive or nice as this."

Hearing this makes my heart hurt, and I wish I could punch Justin's face in for not spoiling her like she deserves. "You're going to love it. There are so many games and books to keep you occupied."

"I've had a smartphone, but this is a totally different level of entertainment."

"Yeah, it really is. I'll show you how to use it if you want."

Tatum is like a kid on Christmas as she opens the iPad box. "Justin got me one years ago. It was his way of buying my forgiveness and silence after one of his rages, and I stupidly bought into it. But it felt so dirty, I never wanted to use it."

Somehow, that doesn't surprise me. It's typical narcissistic behavior.

"Well, this one comes with no conditions. I promise."

"I know. I'm not used to that." She shrugs, and I can tell she doesn't want to keep thinking about it.

"My favorite part is peeling the plastic off," I tell her.

She carefully lifts the tablet and sets it on the counter. "It looks so fancy. The quality has really changed since I last used one."

I smile at her excitement but also feel sadness and anger that she spent years being with a man who didn't treat her well and manipulated her instead.

"You can use my Apple ID to log in and have access to all my apps and books. Just don't look in my *adult folder*."

She looks up at me with wide eyes.

"I'm joking."

She holds her stare.

"Okay, well maybe not." I wink, then log in my email and password so she can get started setting it up how she wants.

I take the laptop out of the bottom of the box and find a few accessories. An extra-long cable for me and a charging cord for Tatum, a pencil for her tablet, and a few cases. She plugs it into one of the extra outlets on the side of the breakfast nook, then carefully peels the plastic from the top. "Yeah, that was pretty satisfying."

"Told you," I tease.

"Will you please give Piper a million thank-yous? This will help distract me for a while, at least." She smiles.

"I think she'd be happy with just one." I grin. "But yes, I will."

"Well then, make it a million and one."

I accidentally drop the cable on the floor, and Tatum jumps again, but I can't ignore it this time. "You okay?"

"Yeah, sorry. Just paranoid, I guess. The windows could give anyone a view inside. You have no idea how insane my ex is."

I stand and close the blinds to make her a little more comfortable for the moment. Considering he burned down my shop, I kinda do.

A side smile sweeps across my lips. "Don't apologize. It's fine. Just know that this place is very secure. Outside cameras cover every angle of the house. Each window has a sensor, and an alarm will go off if it's broken or left open. The doors do too. This house is built like a fortress, and there are alarms for everything. If something happens or anyone tries to break in, we'll know, and the authorities will be alerted right away. You're safe here, Tatum. I *promise*."

She swallows hard. "Thank you. That helps to know. I still have a lot to work through, and seeing him brought it back to the surface."

"A shitty chain of events for sure, but at least you're in good company."

She chuckles. "Thanks for listening. Though I love my sister to death, it feels good to talk to someone else."

"I'm always here to listen."

Before I open the laptop, I FaceTime Piper. As soon as she picks up, she giggles and smiles wide.

"So on a scale from one to ten, how surprised were you?"

"Uhh…ten. As was Tatum. She told me to tell you thank you a million and one times."

"She's so welcome! I hope she enjoys it. There should've been a gift card in the box for her to load it up with games, movies, books—whatever she wants!"

"Shit, I didn't see that," I say, looking in the box again. "Found it."

I hand it to Tatum. "That's too much. You're going to make me cry."

"You're going to need stuff to do while you're stuck with Easton for God knows how long."

"Thanks," I deadpan.

"I mean, I love your brother and thought he was hot as hell, but he's not *that* entertaining." Piper shrugs unapologetically.

Tristan mumbles something in the background.

"Seriously, though, thank you. I needed this so much. Tatum is super appreciative as well."

"Just promise if you need anything else, you'll call. We're happy to help you get your life back together."

"I will."

"Okay, now go fall in love or something."

"Bye, Piper," I say firmly between gritted teeth since I know Tatum heard that. Piper has no idea how I've always felt about Tatum. It's something I've kept buried deep inside. After learning more about her situation, getting into a new relationship could complicate her life even more.

"That house is magical," she hurries and says before ending the call.

"Piper gave me a thousand-dollar gift card," Tatum mutters as she stares at it.

"That's nothing to Piper, trust me. She loves helping others."

"I just don't feel like I deserve this. I'm practically a stranger to her."

"By the time you leave here, you two could be best friends. She has a way with people," I say, then we move to the living room.

I sit on the opposite end of the couch, and every once in a while, when I look up over my screen, I meet her baby-blue eyes.

Once I download a few apps on my laptop, I make a to-do list, and I feel overwhelmed all over again.

"You have that look on your face," Tatum says.

"Which one?" I ask.

"When you're frustrated or deep in thought, your brows furrow, and your lips turn into a firm line like this." She mocks my expression, which makes me laugh.

"Guess I didn't realize I was doing that, but now I do." I go to another tab on the browser. "I'm gonna have to contact a few of my suppliers. Getting ahold of them during the busiest season of the year is gonna be a nightmare."

She sits up a little straighter. "I'll help you with some of this, Easton. I'm patient and have a great customer service voice. Just tell me who to contact, and I'll take care of it. It's the least I could do after everything you've done for me. Let me be useful."

I smile, appreciating her offer because I could really use the extra help. "Alright, I'm happy to take you up on that offer. Keep track of how much time you spend on the phone so I can pay you."

Tatum rolls her eyes. "I owe *you*."

"No, you don't. If you're working, you're getting compensated. "

"Okay, fine." Tatum isn't one to argue, especially when she knows I have *her* best interest in mind.

"Considering how frustrating these vendors are, I feel like your hourly wage should be doubled."

"Nah, I'm up for the challenge. I'll sweet-talk them just like I did you when I needed a job."

I bark out a laugh. "Well, if it worked on me, then I have no doubt it'll work on them."

CHAPTER SIX

TATUM

DAY 4

I'LL NEVER GET tired of seeing the sunrise from my bed. The orange ball peeks over the horizon, and pink, blue, and purple bursts splash across the sky. I climb out from under the blankets and watch it reflect over the water.

I open a window, take in the salty fresh air, and enjoy the way it feels against my bare skin. With such amazing weather, I'm dying to go outside. After I run through my morning routine and get dressed, I go downstairs. As soon as my toes touch the sand, I smile. Though the circumstances of why I'm here are shitty, I really am happy to be here with Easton. I've read stories of other women who've gone through the same thing as me, and many didn't get a second chance at life.

I gave myself to the person I thought Justin was, but I fell in love with someone he wasn't. He could turn his emotions on and off in a snap, and to this day, I'm not sure he ever truly loved me. Rather, he loved the idea of me and what he could do to control me. Though, sometimes I like to think in the beginning he did, even if he manipulated me with gifts.

Because of him, I second-guess everyone's intentions and often forget good people still exist in the world.

I close my eyes and focus on the sound of the waves crashing.

Meditation has saved me in so many ways. I've learned how strong my mind is regardless of how many times Justin tried to break me.

One. Two. Three. Four. Five.

I breathe out slowly, emptying all the air in my lungs before inhaling at the same steady rate. My thoughts move inward as I reflect on the past week, and I hope I can continue to stay mentally strong even though my worst nightmares have come true.

"*Tatum!*" I hear my name being called from behind. My eyes bolt open, and I turn to see Easton walking toward me in a panic.

"Is everything okay?" I ask, trying to figure out what's wrong.

He comes closer and smiles. "Yes, but I was worried about you."

I tilt my head and peer into his green eyes. "Why?"

"Because you ran off without saying anything or letting me know. I almost had a heart attack. I'm not even thirty!"

A laugh releases from me, and I try to cover it but can't seem to wipe the smile from my lips. I find his concern so adorable. "I'm sorry. I didn't want to wake you. Wanted to start my day off right and enjoy the sunrise. First meditation. Second is yoga." I stand and stretch, loosening my shoulders and lower back from sitting.

"Tell me the truth. Do you actually like yoga?"

"Yeah, have you ever done it before?"

He smirks. "No. It always looked way too easy."

I roll my eyes. "Is that cockiness I hear?"

"From me? No. I've just seen all those basic Karens on the beach doing yoga without any problems."

I chew on the edge of my lip. "Alright, tough guy. I think today is the day you learn a little basic bitch yoga."

Easton smirks. "I'm game. Let me go get a towel and some bottles of water for us."

"Perfect, you're gonna need it."

He backs away, showing me his perfect smile, then runs toward the house. Sometimes, I see the way Easton's eyes meet mine and how he allows silence to linger for just a second after I speak. He listens and cares, though he can be tough at times, especially at work.

As I wait for him, I think about what led us here, and it makes me wonder why he's still single. There's not been one woman at the shop or his apartment, at least none that he's shown interest in. At twenty-eight, I'd been married for six years and was living a nightmare of a life.

Easton returns, and he's carrying everything he promised.

"You should stretch first," I tell him, touching my toes. After feeling my quads loosen a bit, I cross one arm over my chest and hold it tight before switching to the other.

"Hope it gets harder than this."

"I'll try to go easy on you," I taunt.

"Oh, okay. Thanks," he says, playfully rolling his eyes.

"First off, we're going to start with three poses—cat, child's, and cobra. We'll go slow, then flow into each one." I show him how to do them all with the correct posture.

"These feel good," he admits when we're in child's pose with our heads down and arms spread in front of us. My legs are tucked, and I feel the stretch. We hold for twenty seconds before moving to the next one.

Once we're finished with those, Easton glances at me. "That's it?"

I sit, then push my legs straight in front of me and slightly lean. "As you exhale, bend your knees, lifting your thighs to a forty-five-degree angle, then straighten your legs, keeping your arms pointing forward. This is cobra." My stance is flawless.

Easton tries but can't seem to straighten his legs without tipping backward.

I lift a brow at him. "We're still in the *intermediate* category."

Seeing him struggling with his big bulky muscles makes me snicker.

"Okay, next one," I tell him. "This is what we call bow." I lie flat on my stomach, then reach behind me and grab the top of my feet with my hands before inhaling. I carefully lift my upper body and open my chest. "Stay lifted for five full breaths to get the full effect."

Easton can't grab the tops of his feet.

"Aw, looks like you need a strap to help you like a basic bitch on the beach."

"Hush." He snickers. "Is it me, or do I have T-Rex arms?"

"It's all those big muscles getting in your way. Just waiting for you to admit that maybe yoga isn't the easiest exercise out there."

"Not yet," he says, being a stubborn Belvedere like Piper said.

"Suit yourself." Moving to my next position, I squat, then place my hands on the ground. Easton follows my every move, and when I lift my hips and bring my knees toward my upper arms, he curses.

"This is crow," I say, keeping my balance steady as I move my feet upward toward my butt. "This is crane."

I hold it for ten more seconds before slowly putting my feet back on the ground.

"After you…" I linger, realizing he's not in the correct position.

Moving closer, I touch his knee. "Spread them wider."

He bursts into laughter, and I almost crack with him.

"Mm-hmm, now put your feet together before lifting yourself. You've got the strength and balance. Just have to put them together," I encourage.

When he lifts himself, I place my hand on his lower back to steady him. "Now lift your legs."

Easton falls to the ground and plops down on his back, laughing. "Shit."

His green eyes meet mine, and I grin.

"This is advanced?"

"No," I say matter-of-factly. "Still intermediate."

We go through different forms of planks, which he totally nails, and the eagle pose before moving to harder ones.

"I dunno if I should warn you or just go for it," I offer.

"Not sure I like the sound of that."

I shrug, well aware that Easton is staring at me as I stand. "Hope you're ready."

"I was born ready."

"Okay, smart-ass." I bend over and walk my hands behind my ankles, then carefully lower my legs onto the back of my upper arms before lifting my feet and pointing my toes straightforward.

"Waiting," I tell him, holding myself up like it's easy. It's not, and it took me two months of practicing to do it without falling, but I don't tell him that.

"Sure," he states, landing flat on his ass. I lower myself and shake out my muscles so I can watch him struggle.

"Is that sweat on your brow?" I taunt.

"Just glistening, like a delicious donut." He tries again and holds it for two seconds before losing his balance. His brows are furrowed, but he doesn't throw in the towel.

"Let's move on." I rotate my wrists. "Now, you're gonna start in a plank, but it's important to warm up your wrists so we're going to shift our body weight forward and back."

After we're done with that, I point my fingertips toward me, and Easton follows. I reach over and move his wrists farther apart.

"Walk your feet back into a plank and bend your elbows, then lean as far forward as you can." My feet lift off the ground, and my body is suspended, straight as a board. This is one of the hardest poses I've ever mastered, and I can't hold it as long as the others. Easton falls forward.

He bursts into heavy laughter, and I notice the way his heart rate ticks in his neck. He rolls onto his back, and I lie next to him, looking up at the clouds rolling overhead.

"So are you ready to admit that yoga kicked your ass?"

"Nah." He turns and looks at me. Our faces are mere inches apart. The smell of his sweat mixed with the fresh scent of his soap lingers, and I find myself thinking about things I shouldn't. There's something in Easton's gaze, something I can't quite make out, and I wonder if I'm imagining the way he looks at me.

I arch a brow, and he shrugs. "Just a little practice, and I'll be a pro."

"Riiiiiiight." The sun is higher in the sky, and I wipe the sweat from my forehead. Though we've only been going for an hour, I know I'll be sore tomorrow. It's been a while since I've done so many poses that use different muscle groups.

"Guess we should go inside before it gets too hot." I feel sweaty all over now that I'm no longer moving.

Easton stands and holds out his hand for me. I grab it, but he uses too much strength, and I stumble into him.

I look up into his eyes. Our breaths and sweat mix as the warm breeze brushes against our skin, and for a brief second, I wonder how soft his lips are.

"My fault. I hulked ya." He laughs, then grabs our towels. We slowly make our way back to the beach house, our arms brushing together as we walk. I love being with Easton because he doesn't force me to talk or try to entertain him. There is no awkwardness in our silence, and I appreciate it more than he knows because I like not having to say anything.

"That was fun," I admit when we step inside. "But now I'm starving."

"I'll make breakfast," he offers, moving to the kitchen.

"Let me." I open the fridge and pull out the eggs and bacon.

Easton grabs two plates, then makes some coffee. He fills a mug and hands it over while watching me cook. His lower back is pressed against the counter.

"You don't trust my cooking, do you?"

I can't help but laugh. "Not sure how to say this, but yeah. No more olives and jalapeños in my breakfast."

"It would be hard for me to fuck up eggs and bacon, though."

"But if anyone could, it'd be you," I add, poking fun at him.

"I'm hurt." He holds his hand over his heart. "But you're not wrong."

"While I'm not picky, I do like my bacon crispy but not burnt," I explain.

After I've put our food on plates, we move to the table and eat. Though it's a huge space, Easton sits beside me.

"I like to look at the beach while I eat," he says, scooting even closer. Easton takes a bite of his eggs and moans. "Guess you're on breakfast duty from here on out."

"Perfect, considering it's my favorite meal of the day."

We fall silent for a few minutes, staring outside.

"Since you showed me some yoga today, I think tomorrow is the day you surf."

I nearly choke on my food. "So soon?"

"Yeah," he says with a chuckle.

"Not sure how much fun it'll be teaching. I could just watch."

"Nice try. We'll get up at dawn."

I find myself staring at his lips, then meet his gaze. "And I'll wear the bathing suit you conveniently got me?"

His smile widens. "I anticipated you'd want to get in the water, but you'll want to wear the bikini bottoms along with the rash guard."

I smirk. "How presumptuous of you."

Easton points outside. "With water like that in your backyard, I was thinking ahead."

"You weren't wrong," I admit, actually looking forward to spending the day with him.

After he takes his last bite of eggs, Easton puts his dirty dishes in the sink. I finish my bacon, and he slides my plate up too.

"I can't wait to see you moving across the waves."

"Glad you believe in me," I tell him. "You might get annoyed with my lack of skills."

His face softens. "I'll be as patient with you as you were with me today."

"Dammit," I mutter. "I'm gonna be screwed."

He chuckles, placing his hand on my shoulder. "Just try to have fun. I'm a good teacher."

"I'm going to hold you to it."

Easton answers his ringing phone, which gives me time to

gather my list. Today, I'm calling vendors, and I'm actually looking forward to focusing on something else.

Easton looks over my list and adds a few more tasks. I make my way to the kitchen table so I can look at the waves while I chat on the phone. I grab my cell and am immediately put on hold.

After a few hours, Easton makes me a sandwich. He brings George into the kitchen and sets him on the table for me to watch. I love this little fur ball more than he realizes. I take a quick break and watch him eat a treat, then get back to it.

Trying to contact people on a Sunday was somewhat silly but worth trying. He warned me it would be annoying, but I guess I have more patience than him. Could be from years of living with a psychopath. When I look down at what I accomplished, I don't feel like I made the best progress, but it was a step in the right direction.

Around five, Easton closes his laptop and meets me at the table.

"I was able to contact two of your sales reps. The others weren't in the office, so I left a lot of voicemails."

He gives me a smile. "Thank you. I really appreciate it. It will be a relief to get this stuff to my insurance agent."

"I'll try again this week," I promise, and he thanks me again.

"I'm going out to the garage to see what boards are out there. Wanna join me?"

I nod and follow him outside. Several boards hang against the wall, and he pulls one down. Easton looks over it, then sets it on a worktable that's off to the side.

"This one will be yours," he says, rubbing his hand across the wood. He pulls another one down for himself. "It's gonna take a little work to get it ready, but we can do it in the morning."

I suck in a deep breath, and he glances at me.

"I feel kinda dumb admitting this, but I'm actually nervous."

His expression softens. "Do you trust me?"

"Yes," I whisper. "I do."

CHAPTER SEVEN

EASTON

DAY 5

An hour before the sun rises, I'm awake and ready to hit the waves. George greets me as he takes his morning jog on the wheel. I go over to his cage and say hello, then stretch with a yawn. I warned Tatum that we'd be up bright and early, but she didn't blink twice when I told her the time.

I'm ready to teach her everything I know and hope she loves my hobby. Yesterday, though it was hard for me to admit, I realized how damn hard yoga really is. Sure, I had my opinions, but it's different when you try to do it. Tatum made it look easy as hell.

I go to her door and knock. To my surprise, it swings open, and she's dressed in the rash guard and swimsuit bottoms.

"It fits perfectly," I say, my eyes scanning over her beautiful body.

She grins. "It really does. I love how it hugs me."

"Luckily, I can look at any person and guess their correct size. I have a ninety-five percent accuracy rate."

She snorts, and I find it cute. "It also helped that I told you what size I wear in everything else."

"We won't mention that part." I chuckle.

We head to the garage, and I grab the supplies we need.

"I'm going to quickly scrape off this old wax and apply some new. Want to do your board?"

A smile touches her lips. "Sure."

I move beside her and hand her the scraper, then plug in the old blow dryer I use to melt the gunk when the sun isn't out.

"So you'll heat the wax just a little, then use this tool to remove all of the old. Once you're done with that, we'll move to the next step."

She takes the blow dryer and guides it across the board, not staying on one spot too long. After it's soft, she starts scraping. "This is gross."

I chuckle. "Yeah, it can be. These haven't been dewaxed in a very long time. While the beach house was being remodeled, I surfed closer to the shop."

"You have more boards than this?" She pushes the scraper down hard, doing an amazing job of clearing the sludge.

"Oh yeah. Too many, actually." I start warming the wax on mine, then do the same. When her board is clean, I hand her a rag and some liquid remover to make sure it's spotless. She meticulously wipes over it, taking her time.

"I had no idea this one was white," she says with a laugh.

"It probably should've been done a long time ago. But now, it's time to apply the new wax."

"What does it do exactly?"

"It helps your feet stick to the board. Otherwise, it's slippery as fuck. It's why you have to scrape off the old and put on new because it loses its tackiness."

"Wow, I had no idea," she admits. "That's interesting."

I love that she's asking questions and seems intrigued by the process. There haven't been a lot of women in my life who ever cared to try. Having someone to surf with on a regular basis would be cool, and I'm hoping she wants to continue learning after today.

"So you're gonna do crisscross lines like this with the wax. Then go back over it in the opposite direction. You'll go up and down it two to three times to make a grid." I hand her the bar after I've done the first pass. Our fingers brush against one another's, and I feel the electricity streaming between us. I'm pretty sure she feels it too, but neither of us mentions it.

When she's done, I show her how to do the circular motions next. "You might use this entire bar. If you do, the drawer over there has several more. You'll want a solid base coat so don't be afraid to use it all."

"Like this?" she asks.

"Exactly," I encourage, going back to mine and making quick work of it.

Randomly, I'll glance at her and smile. She returns the gesture. Every once in a while, I'll sneak a peek and watch her, but she's so focused she doesn't notice.

When Tatum's completed the task, I look over her work, pleased. "Wow, you're going to have a solid grip. You did an awesome job."

"Really?" Her voice goes up an octave like she's shocked.

"Yeah, seriously. I think you did better than me. Guess it's time to hit those waves."

She swallows hard, and I place my hand on her shoulder. "Trust me."

"I do," she repeats, just as she did the day before.

"Actually, I'm gonna leave my board here for a while. I already checked the current and surf so we should be good to go. The sun should be rising any minute, which means we should get a nice show on the horizon."

She grins. "I can't wait. I think the sunrises are the best part of this place. I look forward to them each day."

"Yeah, it's a paradise. That view is why my parents purchased the place all those years ago. It wasn't this nice, but it was ours, and I have a lot of good memories of coming here as a kid."

"I envy you."

I shoot her a grin. "You're welcome to visit anytime you want after we leave. Seriously."

We head toward the beach, and when our feet hit the sand, I breathe in the fresh air as the sun peeks over the horizon. I hold the board, allowing Tatum to take it all in. She stands close, and I'm tempted to take her hand in mine.

"It's beautiful," she whispers as the sky fills with bursts of orange and purple. Fluffy clouds float in the distance as the colors transition from pink to blue.

"Ready?" I ask.

"I guess!"

In the sand, I draw a replica of the board she'll be using. She looks at me like I'm crazy.

"I thought we were going into the water?" Her confused expression makes me laugh.

"Not yet. We're going to practice the basics here first. Hope you're ready to get dirty."

"I look forward to it," she snaps back in a seductive tone that has my cock throbbing.

Once I have the shape in the sand, I draw a line straight down the middle and go through the different areas of the board. I point out the nose and tail—the front and back—so we can use the correct terminology.

"This is the stringer." I motion to the line that goes straight down the middle. When you get to the point of popping up, you'll want your nondominant foot in the middle of it. Your dominant goes behind you."

Tatum gives me a puzzled look like I just asked her to solve a calculus problem.

"Which foot do you naturally kick a soccer ball with?" I ask.

Taking a second, she thinks about it. "My right."

"That one goes behind you because you'll have the most control of the board with it."

I draw myself the same shape, then plop down on my stomach on top of it. She follows my lead.

"Can you swim? I just realized I never asked."

"No," she tells me, and my smile falls.

"Tatum, I didn't reali—"

"I'm kidding." She bursts into laughter. "The look on your face was priceless, though. Of course I can swim. It's just that the ocean is intimidating because I've only gone ankle deep. I swam in tons of pools as a kid, but considering where I grew up, we didn't have anything like this."

I lift a brow. "We're essentially popping your ocean cherry?"

"Something like that." She gives me a toothy grin. "So take good care of me."

"I will. We're not doing white water takeoffs just yet."

"See, sounds intimidating as hell."

"I'm a good teacher. Patient. Good looking. And *well* experienced."

She shakes her head, but her happy expression doesn't falter.

"The goal is to activate your muscles so you're warmed up when we get out there." I make the swimming motions over the sand, and she does too. "You'll want to practice paddling, putting your hands firmly on the deck, then lifting your chest to get to your feet. Let's go through it a few times."

I demonstrate so she understands the movements. "Paddle, palms, lift, pop," I say in a way that's easy to understand. "Keep your feet shoulder-width apart when you finally stand."

"It's like a freakin' burpee without the hop," she tells me.

I chuckle. "Yeah, I guess it is. Never thought of it like that. Just remember the dominant foot goes behind you, and your front one should have the stringer going through the middle." I point at the board to remind her. It can be a lot of information to take in at once, but Tatum practices until she's got it down.

"Why are you smiling?" she asks, dusting off the sand that's stuck to her body.

"Because I know a natural when I see one."

"You're the best hype squad ever," she admits.

I place my hand on her shoulder and gently squeeze.

"I think we're ready for the water."

"Already?"

"Yep," I say, picking up the board and walking toward it.

She steps in and stops when we're at her calf. "How far are we going?"

"About ten more feet from where you are. Waist-deep only."

Her shoulders relax.

"For now," I add with a wink and wave her toward me. "When you carry the board into the water, you'll want to point the nose toward the wave and lift it so the wave travels under."

"Got it," she tells me, watching.

Beginners usually use the leg rope attached to the wood, but since I'm here, I won't let it escape me so there's no need. "The goal is for you to find the sweet spot. You'll hop on and scoot your body around, making sure you're not too far forward or back. It's all about balance, and after yesterday, we both know you're good at that."

"True."

"Climb on," I say, patting it. "I'll hold it steady for you."

She starts from the back, and I keep a tight grip so it doesn't shoot out from under her. Thankfully, the water's calm, something that makes learning less scary.

"Good job," I praise. "Now when you're too far forward, the nose sinks. When you're too far back, the tail sinks and the nose pops up, making it difficult to stay on. So you'll want to move around until it feels level. Each board is different so you have to find the right spot for you. When you're positioned correctly, you'll know."

Her hair is wet and sticks to her forehead. Tatum almost instantly discovers the balance point. As I grip the side, I can't help but stare at her beautiful ass. She doesn't even try to pull down the material, and I wish I could revel in her. A part of me wonders if she likes me looking.

"How's that?" I finally ask.

"Comfortable," she says with a grin. "Is this where I should be?"

Her doe eyes meet mine, and I nod. "Yep, this is it. So now we'll do what we practiced on the sand, but I want you to feel how a wave pushes you along without standing."

I glance behind me, seeing the perfect one coming. "Are you ready to paddle?"

She nods just as the fluffy white water heads toward us.

"Go," I say, and Tatum starts moving her arms. The water catches her perfectly and pushes her along. I can hear her laughing as it nearly brings her to shore. She rolls off, smiling wide.

"That was amazing!" She stands and comes back to me with the board in hand.

"And you haven't even stood yet," I say, and her excitement is contagious. I remember the first time I soared across the water and felt the same way.

"When you paddle, try to keep your legs together so you'll have more control. Once the wave carries you, that's when you know it's time to stand."

"I think I understand."

"Want to go again? It's best to ride some waves on your stomach a few times to get used to the feel of it. Once you're comfortable, we'll try the pop-up."

She nods. "Sounds great. I'm so excited. This is actually fun."

I turn and look at the oncoming waves. "Okay, take it. Hop on and start paddling."

Tatum does exactly what I say. She's zooming across the water fully enjoying herself, and it makes me so damn happy. I've never had a woman love being out here with me or even remotely pretend to enjoy it.

When she returns, she's ecstatic. She goes a few more times, riding all the way to the shore then coming back, and I know she's getting tired. Between the sun and the waves, and adding the physical aspects, it will beat you down.

"Want to take a short break? Maybe grab a snack and water to refuel? I don't want you getting dehydrated."

"Yes, that sounds great."

"Here comes your wave. I'll meet you on the sand," I say, and she goes for it. This time, she tries to stand but loses her balance and falls over.

I meet up with her. "You were so damn close."

She's breathing heavily. "It felt good, but I just need to get my feet right."

"There will be plenty of time for that." I shoot her a wink. Grabbing the board from her, I carry it under my arm as we go back to the house.

"I can't believe I've never tried this before. And I probably wouldn't have without you talking me into it," she admits. "I just never knew where to start."

"You're actually doing really great. It's impressive."

I think I see a hint of a blush hit her cheeks as we grab a few towels and quickly dry off, then go inside. The air-conditioning is cool on my skin as I grab a few bags of chips, a couple of bottles of water, and make some ham sandwiches. We devour them quickly, and Tatum is itching to go back.

"You know, my mother used to tell me that I had to wait an hour before I got in the water after eating."

"Is there a reason?"

I laugh. "No. I think it's something to tell kids so they don't throw up from doing too much. I never listened and never puked. So I'm ready when you are."

Before we return, I grab my board and grab water bottles so we have plenty to drink. The sun is out, and it's easy to get dehydrated, even if it's not midday yet.

Tatum carries hers, and before we walk out into the ocean, I show her how to put the strap on her ankle. "It goes on the nondominant foot. That way, if you fall off, it won't drift away and stay close to you."

"That's nifty," she admits, bending down and attaching it. "You're gonna surf with me?"

"Yep, I'll keep watch and tell you when to stand."

"Great," she says, giving me a wink. There are so many unspoken words, and I can't deny the chemistry that's always been there. Seeing her so free and happy like this makes me want to take her on new adventures to experience things she hasn't yet.

Once we're waist-deep, I turn and watch, then hop on my board when the opportunity arises. Tatum follows, and we paddle hard. Once the wave catches and begins to push us, I tell her to pop up.

"Now!" I call out and do it with her. When I look over, her feet are on the board, and though she's unsteady, she's zooming straight across the water.

"Amazing!" I shout, meeting up with her when she jumps off.

"I didn't release the board and fully stand until my legs were completely in place. It made it easier though I still felt wonky."

I give her a high five but really want to pull her into my arms. I'm so proud. "That's exactly right! Keep your upper body a little lower next time. Sometimes, that makes it easier to control until you're more comfortable balancing."

"Okay!" She races back out. The next few times, she falls off before fully standing, but after an hour of practicing, she's got it down perfectly.

"Slightly bend the knees and look where you want to go," I yell, surfing close, studying her stance. The smile on her face doesn't falter.

After a while, we take another break, setting our boards down and sitting on the sand.

"Thank you," she tells me, chewing on her bottom lip.

"Thank *you*. This has been a lot of fun."

"It really has. I think I might have a new hobby to obsess about. I mean, I work in a surf shop after all."

A roar of laughter escapes me. "That you do. I really think if you kept up with it, you could start riding unbroken waves."

Her eyes widen. "And that means what exactly?"

"You don't wait for the white water. You start off before the wave breaks and take off at an angle."

"Will you show me?"

"Sure." Grabbing my board, I swim into the deep water, then sit on my board and wait. In the distance, I see the perfect wave building and paddle. Before it breaks, I ride it at an angle. The board glides across the water like it's glass, and I show off by switching my positions, knowing Tatum is watching. Once I've ridden it to the end, I meet her on the sand.

"Wow, I think I might be speechless." She's grinning as she looks up at me and shields her eyes from the sun.

"You'll get there," I say confidently.

"That would be amazing. I'd love it if we could do this again sometime."

"I'm ready when you are. There's something special about being out there that's hard to describe." I hold out my hand to help her up. She dusts the sand off her perfect ass.

"I get it. I've always been obsessed with the ocean. It's why when I left my ex, Florida was the only place I could imagine starting a new life."

"I hope you do," I mutter, meaning it. "You'll always have a place to work and live."

"Thanks. That means a lot."

We take our boards to the garage and place them back on the wall. Then I lead her to the outdoor shower. "Might want to rinse off before going inside," I say, opening the door. "You can keep your clothes on."

"I planned on it." She steps in, and it takes her a few minutes. Once she's finished, I jump in.

"I think I want to take a hot bubble bath," she admits when we go inside.

"You should. You'll probably be sore tomorrow."

"After yoga yesterday and surfing today, I might not be able to walk tomorrow."

I pop a brow, and the thought has my mind wandering. "Enjoy."

"I'll start on dinner when I'm done."

Our eyes meet, and it seems like she wants to say something more but doesn't.

While Tatum finishes with her bath, I take a shower. After an hour, she comes downstairs dressed and looking sexy as always, but then I notice she's just as sunburned as I am. I realized we forgot sunscreen as soon as I got in the shower.

When she sits at the opposite end of the couch, I can tell something is wrong. Her demeanor has drastically changed from an hour ago.

"Everything okay?"

Tatum shakes her head. "I just got this weird text message."

I scoot closer to her, and she hands over her phone. It's a local number based on the area code, but not one I recognize.

Unknown: Hope you're having fun. Enjoy it while you can.

I read it, and while it seems threatening, it could be a wrong number.

"I think it's my ex." Her hand shakes as she reads it again. I don't like seeing her so worked up, but I also wouldn't put it past Justin. Right now, I want to comfort her.

"It *could* be a wrong number because it's local. I get weird texts all the time," I admit.

"Things like this?" She locks her phone.

"No, but that doesn't matter. It does happen."

"He won't stop until I'm dead, Easton. He won't." A sob

escapes her, and I hold out my arms. At first, she hesitates, but then she falls into them.

I hold her tight and pet her wet hair, trying to calm her. "I won't ever let that happen. Ever. You're safe here with me, Tatum."

No matter what, I don't let go, not until she makes the decision to pull away. When she does, I brush my thumbs across her cheeks, wiping away the tears. "Have you called your lawyer yet?"

"No, but I will. I need to. I hoped that I could just ignore all of this, and it'd go away. This is proof it won't." After sucking in a few deep breaths, Tatum excuses herself to make the call. I'm so angry that this man still has so much power over her.

Twenty minutes later, she returns, and I can tell she's been crying again.

"He thinks getting a temporary restraining order on Justin needs to happen, especially since he's searching for me. He stressed how important it is to have a paper trail of these things in case it escalates."

"I agree. We can go on Wednesday if that works for you."

"Sounds great." She doesn't sound enthused. "I'm not your problem, but here we are again."

"Tatum," my voice softens. "You're not a problem, period."

"You keep saying that, but it doesn't change the way I feel. If you knew all of this would happen the day you met me, would you change it?" She meets my eyes.

"Hell no. Meeting you has been a highlight, and I know that's cheesy as fuck to say. But I mean it." Plus, she's beautiful, charming, and caring.

"That makes me feel a little better. Glad you wouldn't erase my existence if you could."

"Never. I do want to ask you a question," I gently say.

"You can ask me anything."

"Why did you stay with him for so long if he's this insane?"

Tatum sucks in a deep breath, keeping her focus on the floor. "Honestly, I'm not sure."

Tension fills the room, so I change the subject, knowing that's all she's going to give me. "On another note, next time we're outside, we can't forget the sunscreen. Keep doing this, and we'll look like lobsters," I say.

Right now, she's strung so tight, and I just want her to relax.

She laughs. "I hope there is a next time."

"There will be *plenty* of them. Trust me."

A smile touches her beautiful lips, and she tucks loose strands of damp hair behind her ear. "I'd like that a lot. Tomorrow, this will be a nice tan. I usually don't burn. But I'm making a mental note now. Sunscreen." Tatum unlocks her iPad, then flips it around. There's a photo of some chicken breasts surrounded by mushrooms. "I'm cooking this tonight."

"Looks delicious," I admit, just as my cell phone buzzes. I see it's Tristan and excuse myself to chat.

"What's up?" I answer, grinning.

"I should be asking you the same question," he says in his usual serious tone.

"Whatcha mean? Everything's going great. The updates to the house have been a total game changer. Yesterday, Tatum taught me how to do yoga."

He snorts. "I bet that was a sight to see."

"It's a lot harder than I imagined. But today, I gave her a surfing lesson."

"Really?" He sounds surprised. "And she's not trying to escape after that?"

"Actually, no. She's a natural and really loves the water. First woman I've ever met who enjoyed being taught."

"That's great, man. Happy to hear that. Oh, and I called for a reason."

"You typically do," I throw back, but I'm still smiling. I know how he is.

"I'm really concerned about your well-being. Do you have any weapons in the house?"

I pause for a second and think about it. "Only the sharp-ass kitchen knives Piper ordered."

"That's not enough. How would you protect yourself if you were attacked?"

I glance out at the water and chuckle. "Attacked? I'd use a few karate chops and kicks."

Tristan doesn't laugh. "Cute."

"I'm not gonna get attacked. This house is a security fortress. As long as we're here, we're safe."

Tristan clears his throat and sucks in a deep breath. I brace myself for whatever he's about to say. "Yeah, well, Piper was tracked by her phone, and Tatum's could be too. You need to be careful and stay under the radar. Don't go in public. Stop using the internet. Go into complete and utter lockdown."

I roll my eyes and blow him off. "I really think you're worrying too much. If I'm not concerned, you shouldn't be either."

"Too late. How do you think Tatum was found in the first place? How do you think her ex tracked her to your place of business? You're not dealing with some idiot, Easton. You need to wake up before you both get hurt. This is dangerous, and I don't feel like you're taking it seriously."

I scoff. "I am. The last thing I need is you getting on a plane and trying to come act as *my* bodyguard."

"Yeah, well, it didn't help Piper that much, and I'm overqualified. You're in the way of him getting to Tatum, so don't think for a second that you're not his first target. You are."

"Everything will be fine."

He sighs. "I hope so, Easton. Not sure I could live with myself if it's not."

"Is this your way of telling me you love me?" I chuckle.

"Of course I do. You know that."

I hear Piper yell in the background. "I love you too!"

"Okay, let's not get too mushy around here. If things get weird, I'll let you know. But right now, there are no issues." I keep the weird text message Tatum received to myself because it would just set him off on another rant.

"Stay safe, Easton."

"I will," I say, then end the call.

I honestly expected this talk at some point. I just didn't realize it would be so soon.

CHAPTER EIGHT

TATUM

DAY 7

"DID YA BANG HIM YET?" Oakley asks as soon as her face appears on the screen. Even though it isn't Friday, she asked me to call and update her.

"Who?" I play dumb. She doesn't need to know I've thought about it more than once. Justin's and my sex life started out great but quickly went downhill. I still very much desire it, but I shouldn't jump into anything, even if it was just a physical relationship.

"Oh, *please*. You can't fool me. Did you bring your vibrator?"

I roll my eyes. "Fire, remember? I lost everything."

"Oh shit. No problem. I'll send you one. You need some action. What's the address there?"

"You better not...that would be incredibly embarrassing if he saw it."

"It'll be in a discreet package. Doubt he'll even know what it is."

I sigh and tell her the address. "Don't you dare send me a twelve-inch monster dick either."

"Don't worry, sis. I gotchu. Sending you my favorite one. It'll have you screaming Easton's name in thirty seconds, and bonus, it's waterproof."

"Lovely," I deadpan. "Anyway..."

"Okay, ordered! It'll arrive tomorrow."

"Great. Hopefully, Easton doesn't find it."

"You're thirty-seven, gorgeous, and thriving. So if he does, own that shit."

"I think you and I have different definitions of *thriving*."

More like living in complete chaos.

"So any new info?"

"My attorney suggested I file a temporary restraining order. So Easton is taking me to do that today."

"Good, I'm proud of you. Probably should've done that a long time ago, but better late than never," she says.

"I know. I'm nervous to leave the house, though, because Justin's so unpredictable."

"You think he'd do anything with witnesses around?"

I shrug. "Part of me thinks the worst. I wouldn't be surprised if he tried to kidnap me and drag me back to Nebraska."

"Like a true psychopath."

I nod.

"Will you call me when you're back so I know you're safe? I don't have class until this evening, so I'll be around."

"Yeah, of course. I'll probably have to find something to distract myself so I don't overthink everything. The moment Justin gets served, he's going to flip his shit even more."

"Wish I could be a fly on that wall. I'd love to see his stupid face the moment he realizes you're fighting back."

"It won't look good for his career. He'll be pissed." But I

don't care. I'm only concerned about what this will motivate him to do. Retaliation is his middle name.

We chat for a few more minutes, and she gives me some details about one of the classes she's taking. Her chatting about watercolors distracts me until I have to leave.

"I'll text you when I'm safe and sound," I tell her.

"Yes, please do. And Tate?"

"Hm?"

She smiles genuinely. "I'm proud of you. I know this is hard for you, but just know you're doing the right thing. I'm glad Easton's by your side, especially since I can't be."

Me too, I think to myself. I'd be lost without him at this point.

"Thanks, sis. I wish I'd done it a long time ago so it wouldn't have gotten to this point."

"Don't blame yourself for anything that's happened, okay? Had I known how bad it was, I would've been on the first flight there to rescue you."

"That's why I didn't say anything. I wanted to protect you too."

"I understand why you didn't. Justin could've used a royal kick in the dick, though."

I snort. "Okay, I gotta go for real now. Love you."

"Love you too! You got this, sis!" she calls out, then I press the end button.

From the pep talk she gave me, you'd think *she* was the older sibling. But I adore her for it. She's young and hip but is also an old soul.

"Ready?" Easton asks when I come downstairs.

I nod. "As ready as I'll ever be."

He flashes me a cute boyish grin. "We'll be back in our cozy paradise before ya know it."

I blow out a breath. "I hope so."

He casually wraps an arm around my shoulders, pushing me against his hard chest. "Don't worry. I'll be by your side the entire time."

If he only knew what his words did to me.

I clear my throat and my mind. I need to think straight, which is hard when Easton's the most charming and gorgeous man I've ever seen. "Thanks."

Easton drives us into town, which takes about forty-five minutes. About halfway there, he notices my leg bouncing and reaches over to comfort me. I didn't realize I was doing it, but he kept his hand on my thigh even after I stopped—which had my thoughts consumed by something else entirely.

After we park, we walk in and find where we need to go to fill out the paperwork. Though it's only temporary, it gives me a little relief for the time being. As promised, Easton stays glued to my side as I fill out the detailed forms. My hands shake, so it takes me longer, but he doesn't rush me. Instead, he rests his hand on my lower back to remind me he's close. When I glance up, he's looking around and making sure everything's secure. It gives me peace of mind so I can focus on doing this correctly.

Twenty minutes later, we're back in the car, and I stay silent. I can't stop imagining Justin reading those papers. This will confirm I'm in Florida, but I can't let him get away with this any longer, so I'm glad I did it.

I just wish he hadn't put me in this position in the first place.

I wish he would've treated me better, like the loving partner he vowed to be fifteen years ago.

I wish I'd been stronger. To see the signs sooner. To walk away before it had gotten to the point of him completely controlling me.

"Tatum."

Easton's booming voice shakes me out of my head, and I blink over at him.

"We're back," he says.

I glance around and see the beach house.

"You doing okay? You were quiet the whole drive."

I smile and nod, though I'm not sure if the reassurance is for him or me.

"Let's do something fun to get your mind off everything," Easton offers, opening my car door.

"Like what? I'm still sore from my surfing lesson." I grin, following him to the door where he punches in the code. Once we're securely inside, he locks it and sets the alarm.

"Don't worry. There's almost little to no physical activity."

He leads me through the house to the game room. "You know how to play pool?"

"I know the general concept, yes, but I haven't played in years," I admit.

"You wanna do it? I'll even go easy on ya," he mocks with a wink.

I laugh, some of my anxiousness releasing. "Sure. You set up the game. I gotta call Oakley really quick so she doesn't worry."

"You got it, boss."

"Har har."

Easton flashes me his devilish boyish grin. With everything going on in his life and with the shop, he still makes an effort to keep *my* mind occupied.

I walk up to my room and dial my sister's number. She answers on the second ring.

"How'd it go?"

"Actually, it went fine. Easton acted like my personal bodyguard. The nerves were still present, but I didn't worry about anyone coming for me. If they tried, he would've tackled them in two seconds."

"Would it be weird to wish Justin would just so I could see him get his ass beat?"

"*Oakley!*"

"You should let me meet Easton on FaceTime so I can see for myself."

"See what?"

"What's making you drool every day. I think it's my right to be introduced to my future brother-in-law."

"You're ridiculous. I'm hanging up." I glare.

"Wait! Before you go and do God only knows what with him, I just wanted to say that given the circumstances, you've been happier this past week than I've seen you in months, hell, *years*. I hope this version of you is here to stay."

"Thanks, sis. I feel a ton of mixed emotions, but I can definitely say that happiness is somewhere on that list. He showed me how to surf a couple of days ago. That was a ton of fun."

"You? *Surfing?* I can't picture it." She chuckles.

"Sure did. He even said I was pretty good too."

"I bet he did," she sing-songs in her sarcastic tone. "He got a front row seat staring at your bootylicious ass."

I roll my eyes, even though she can't see me, and sigh. The majority of what comes out of my sister's mouth is sass and sarcasm.

"He wasn't looking," I reassure her. "He remained professional the whole time."

"Were you wearing a nun suit?"

"Uh, no. A bikini bottom and swimming shirt."

"Oh then sis, he was *absolutely* checking out your ass. Probably your tits too."

"The last time I had a guy even look my way like that was over a decade ago."

"Based on what you've told me these past two months and how protective of you he's been, I can't imagine him not noticing how gorgeous you are. If Easton's a twentysomething red-blooded man who likes women, he's definitely *noticing*."

"Well, even so, that doesn't mean anything will happen," I remind her. "In fact, any kind of sexual relationship is off the table. I'm not in the market for one."

"If that's the case, maybe you should introduce him to your *very* single and sexy sister."

I snort. "Sure. When you can reassure me you won't jump his bones like a wild bear, I'll get right on that."

She laughs, not giving me the reassurance I need, but I change the subject and let her know he's waiting on me in the game room.

"Gonna play pool, huh? More ways to gawk at your ass."

"Goodbye, you pain in my butt."

"Love you!" she calls out before I end the call.

Her generation seriously has no filter.

"Everything okay?" Easton asks when I return twenty minutes later. "I thought maybe you fell asleep."

"No, Oakley's a chatterbox. You'll find out someday, I'm sure."

"Is she coming to visit?"

"I don't know, but she's been persistent about meeting you. Even if it's through FaceTime."

"So you've been talking me up, huh? What're you telling her?" The corner of his lips tilt up into a shit-eating grin.

"That you can't cook or change out smoke detector batteries, and you have a co-dependent hamster named George. Oddly, that only made her want to meet you even more."

My serious tone causes his jaw to drop, and after a few seconds, I burst out laughing.

"Low blow about George, by the way." He points at me. "But otherwise, accurate."

"It's okay," I coo and smile at his cage. Easton must've brought him in while I was gone. "Most people get attached to their pets, so you aren't much different."

"Well for that little smart-ass remark, you get to break."

I take the pool stick from his grip, rub some chalk on the tip, then line up the shot. As I focus on my aim, my thoughts go back to Oakley's comments about him staring at my ass. As I glance over at him, I notice his gaze wandering to my backside.

"Is there something wrong with my posture?" I ask, bringing his attention to my face.

His gaze snaps to my eyes as he scratches his cheek. "Uh...well, you should spread your legs out a bit more. They should be shoulder-width apart with one foot forward. Lower your chest closer toward the table so you can properly align the stick to the center of the ball." His deep baritone sends shivers down my spine.

I follow his instructions and adjust my stance. When he approves with a nod, I make my shot.

"Not bad."

No balls went in.

"Next time, arch your back and add a little more force."

Easton goes next and sinks two balls. "Guess that means you're stripes." He takes another turn and misses.

I walk around to the other side, trying to find a good angle. The perfect one is in front of him. Instead of moving when I lean over the table, his feet stay planted behind me.

"How's the view from there?" I mock.

"Not bad, but I'd say you need to go lower."

I blink. "Excuse me?"

Easton presses his palm to the small curve of my back. My shirt rose up when I moved. "Like this," he states, pushing me down. "It'll allow you to fully see the playing field."

I gulp as his warm hand presses against my skin. He's made no attempt to remove it.

"Take your shot, stripes." His low, husky tone causes pleasure to shoot between my thighs.

What the hell is happening to me?

After ten seconds of trying to collect myself, I strike the ball and watch as my ball goes straight into the pocket.

"Beautiful," he murmurs.

Slowly, I stand and look over at him.

"Did you feel that?"

I blink a few times, my heart racing a million miles an hour. "W-What?"

"Your posture. How you were able to get the ball in..."

"Yeah. I think I've figured it out now."

He flashes me a wink. "Awesome, let's see you do it again."

I move to the other side of the table, and this time, he stays in place. Putting myself in the same stance, I focus on the cue ball and aim for the middle pocket. My chest rises and falls as I nervously pull back and slam my stick into it. It shoots forward and hits the side of the table, speeding past where it should've gone.

Dammit.

"So close," Easton says.

He knocks two more of his in, then misses the third before it's my turn again. That time I make it but miss the next. We go back and forth until we each have one ball left.

"Okay, stripes. You got this?"

I grin at his teasing tone because my ball is only inches away from the pocket.

"Get ready to lose," I taunt.

Easton lifts his arm and reaches behind his neck for the back of his shirt, then slowly pulls it off. "You're making me sweat with all that confidence." He uses the fabric to wipe off his forehead. My eyes focus on his broad chest and lower to his stomach.

Jesus Christ.

I've seen him shirtless before, but right now, he's close enough to touch and lick that *sweat* off his body.

His playful wink nearly does me in.

I swallow hard and refocus on the game. Sucking in a breath, I take the shot.

And fucking miss.

"You play *dirty*."

"What do you mean? I even taught you the correct stance!" he says innocently. But his smirk isn't fooling me.

I narrow my eyes because he knows exactly what I'm talking about.

"My turn." He walks around to my side, acting like he's already won.

"Your arrogance is showing," I tell him.

"You mean my *optimism*?"

I lick my lips and plant my feet. If he wants this shot, he'll have to do it pressed against me.

"Well, good luck to you then," I say, crossing my arms.

He starts to lower himself, then realizes he needs to move closer to line up the stick.

"Excuse me, please."

"Go ahead." I shrug, and that's when it hits him that I'm playing him right back.

Easton slides into position, and his eyes are level with my

ass. I look back at him, and he's wearing a devilish smirk on his face. Without focusing on the stick or ball, Easton takes his shot. It goes directly into the hole.

"You weren't even looking!" I gasp.

"Trust me, I was." He winks, moves a few inches over, then smashes the eight ball in.

"That's game, stripes. You wanna knock your last one in for sentimental purposes?"

"You're a cocky shit," I groan, stepping around him and tossing it into a pocket. "You're supposed to be a gentleman and let the woman win. It's called *chivalry*."

He barks out a laugh. "I think I found your first flaw. You hate losing."

I furrow my brows. "Don't worry, I have many more than that." *And insecurities too.*

He lowers his eyes like he's memorizing every inch of my body. Usually, being under his hard gaze would make me self-conscious, but for once, I'm not. I wish I could read his mind when he looks at me like that.

"Nope, I only see *sore loser*." He shrugs, and I roll my eyes.

"You're insufferable," I mutter, hanging my stick on the wall.

Easton laughs, setting up the table again. "I've heard that a time or two. You hungry?"

"You cooking?" I lift a brow.

"Hell no. That's apparently *my* one flaw."

I snort, shaking my head as I walk to the kitchen. "C'mon, since you gave me pool tips, it's time I show you how to make real food."

"Omelets *are* real food," he argues.

"Not the way you make them," I say with a chuckle.

Once we're behind the counter, he grabs an apron and ties

it around his waist. He looks ridiculous, but in a *super sexy shouldn't be thinking about my boss* kind of way.

Fuck me.

At least he's taking my mind off my shitstorm life. He's the perfect distraction.

CHAPTER NINE

EASTON

DAY 10

After Tatum's second surf lesson early yesterday, I slept in until nine. She's getting the hang of it, and I enjoy watching her. Each time Tatum stands upright on the board, she grows more confident, and I love seeing her find this new happy version of herself. Every day we try to do something different to pass the time, and honestly, I can't believe a week and a half has passed. Updates from the insurance company and police department have been slow, but since it's Saturday, I won't hear anything until next week.

After lunch, Tatum soaks in the tub, and it takes cleaning the kitchen to distract me from fantasizing about her in there. The lines are blurring more and more each day, but neither of us is ready to admit our underlying feelings. Tatum's going through a major life change, and I don't want to complicate things more, but I'm certain she's giving me the same signs I'm giving her. Tatum wants me as much as I want her.

My phone vibrates, and I find a message from Piper.

Piper: I don't want you to be worried about a strange truck pulling into the driveway, so I'm just letting you know a delivery is coming for you today! It will have instructions, so READ THEM.

She's a bossy little shit, but I smile at her aggressiveness.

Easton: Geez, you sending me a cookbook?

Piper: Nope, 10000x better!

Easton: Not gonna lie, I'm a little scared.

Piper: Make sure Tatum is there! You'll need her help.

My mind goes to a game or a puzzle maybe, but I don't know why she'd be so excited about that.

Easton: Alright, sis. I'll keep a lookout for it, I guess.

Piper: I can't wait!

I have no idea what's up her sleeve, but I never put anything extra or over the top past her.

Ten minutes later, the doorbell rings, and I'm shocked it arrived so soon. I find a brown box on the porch and bring it into the kitchen. There's nothing on the outside to give away what it could be, but it feels light. Now, I'm even more confused.

I rip off the tape just as Tatum walks out with a towel on her head.

"Hey, what's that?"

"I was just about to figure that out. Piper sent it."

Inside is another box, but it's black.

"What do you think it is?" she asks.

"She told me she sent instructions and to have you help me with it, but I don't see any."

Tatum unravels her towel and throws her hair into a wet messy bun. Even undone and fresh out of a bath, she looks stunning.

"Is that it? That little white card," she says, pointing at the other side of the box.

"Oh, it must be." I rip it off and open the envelope.

I hope you like the one I picked out. Take it in the shower with you and imagine your boss's hands and tongue all over you.

Love,

Your absolutely favorite little sister

PS—I included some scented lube ;-)

I blink and swallow hard as I try to come to terms with what the fuck I just read. This can't be from Piper.

"What's it say?" Tatum asks.

"Uh...I'm not sure this package is for me."

"Oh. Who's it for?"

I hand her the note and watch as her eyes nearly bug out of her head. Her palm covers her mouth, and it takes her a few seconds to speak. "Oh my God."

Her cheeks turn a sexy shade of red before she quickly lifts the lid and peeks inside. "I'm going to *die*. After I kill my sister."

"Over a vibrator? Don't most chicks have those?" I ask,

trying to reassure her that she has nothing to be embarrassed about.

"I'm sure they do, but I wasn't referring to that. I cannot believe she wrote that note. Easton, I'm so—"

"Tatum, it's okay. I know how siblings can be. I'm sure she said it to get a reaction out of you. It's no big deal."

I cover her other hand with mine and give it a little squeeze. Whether or not her sister's words are true, I don't want Tatum to feel awkward. It's taken us long enough to be comfortable together, and I'd hate to backtrack. I enjoy her company, but she's still my employee, and we need to maintain professional boundaries.

That's what the logical part of my brain says anyway.

The other part wants me to open that box and use that vibrator on her until she screams my name and comes all over it.

"I'm going to just...take this upstairs. You know, out of sight and out of mind. And then I'm going to drown myself in the ocean. Be right back."

I chuckle at how frazzled she is. Not over the fact that she uses a sex toy but because of her sister's comments about her boss, *me*. If they weren't true, there's no way she'd be acting this way.

It takes Tatum twenty-five minutes to come back downstairs. She's changed her clothes and brushed out her hair, looking pretty as always.

"So?"

"So what?" She furrows her brows as she sits next to me on the couch.

"Did you give your new vibrator a test run?"

She stands, but I quickly grab her wrist and pull her down. "Oh come on, I'm just teasing."

She shoots me a glare, and it causes me to laugh. "How

about I share an embarrassing story with you so we're on an even playing ground? Then you can make fun of me for it all you want."

Tatum folds her arms over her chest and stares at me. "That'll depend on how bad this story is."

I turn my body toward her with a grin. "I had a major crush on a teacher in high school. She was at least ten to twelve years older than me, and it was the first time I realized I was attracted to *older* women. Of course, the circumstances made it a thousand percent illegal, but I needed a way to get my feelings out before I embarrassed myself. So I started writing in a journal. Random thoughts I had, what I noticed about her that day, and that eventually turned into poetry."

"Oh my God," she mutters, holding back a smile. Yeah, she already knows where this is going.

"Halfway through my junior year, she was offering after-school tutoring to five students only. You bet your ass I was first in line. Even though I was acing her English class, I was prepared to dumb myself down just to get her attention."

Tatum looks at me with pity in her eyes and a smile on her lips. My plan to make her feel better is already working.

"My teacher knows I don't need the extra help, so instead, she asks me to help tutor one of the other students after school. Of course, I agree because I wanted any reason to be around her. He was a guy I had trouble with before, and I'd put him in his place a few times. You know the type of prick, a top athlete who talks a lot of shit. While I was taking notebooks from my backpack, my journal fell out, and he grabbed it. Before I could stop him, he opened it and started reading."

"Oh no..." Tatum smirks. "He saw all your private thoughts."

"Yeah, then he read them aloud for everyone else to hear,

even her. I'd stupidly written her entire name in one of my poems so I couldn't even lie about who it was about. He was bigger than me, and I was too chickenshit to fight him. From that point on, I was teased for being in love with our teacher."

"How'd she react?"

"She was humiliated, and so was I. Even worse was when she asked me to stay after, and the other students started a rumor that we were having an affair. News spread *fast*. Whispers about me echoed through the halls. I did my best to ignore them, but then a week later, the principal and counselor brought me into the office. They asked if I was being sexually abused or taken advantage of by a teacher. Of course I said no, but they got a hold of the notebook and used it as evidence against her. Some things I wrote were...*graphic*. Fantasies. With details. All in my sixteen-year-old head. They thought it was legit. The school placed her on leave while they decided what to do. Once they chose to take it to court, I had to testify and explain my fascination with her in great detail to prove that she'd never touched me."

She slowly shakes her head in disbelief as I feel that humiliation all over again.

"Okay, you win. That is *insane!*" She gasps.

"Her husband was ready to murder me. Even though she was found not guilty, it turned their lives upside down. By the time it was over, the whole town knew what happened, and she ended up moving across the country. I'd apologized profusely, but the damage was done. I learned a valuable lesson—never write down your feelings," I say with a chuckle.

"Or tell your sister you have a younger, single, good-looking boss. Always comes back to bite you in the ass."

I arch a brow. "You think I'm good looking, huh?"

She rolls her eyes. "As if you didn't already know you are. I didn't say that was my type," she retorts.

THE HEART OF US

"How is it not? Well, that could explain some things, actually..." I taunt, nudging her shoulder.

"Oh, shush. Truthfully, who knows what my type is anymore."

"With my luck, you're into old guys who wear white New Balance sneakers with knee-high socks."

Tatum laughs until tears roll down her cheeks.

"Thanks."

"For what?" I ask.

"Easing my embarrassment. Not that I'm happy you went through that, but I appreciate you sharing it with me. Now I need to plot how to get Oakley back."

"I'm sure you'll think of something."

Moments later, the doorbell chimes, and this time, I know the package is mine since I actually checked the label.

"So that's from Tristan and Piper?" she asks as I set it on the coffee table.

"Yep." I find an envelope with the instructions on top of a box and rip it open. I read the note aloud.

Easton, there are five gifts, and each one is numbered. You must open them in order, then read the second card last. Make sure Tatum records it all, then send it to me ASAP!
Love, the best sister-in-law you'll ever have

"Her generation has to video everything, I swear," Tatum says with a chuckle as I hand her my cell phone.

"She's not that much younger than me, but yeah. They came out of the womb with the ability to text before they could talk."

"And go." She points the lens toward me.

"Here's gift number one." I hold it up, then unwrap it. "Ooh, a candle." I smell it before placing it under Tatum's nose.

"Smells like baby powder or fresh linen," she says, and I agree.

"Alright, gift number two is..." I tear the paper. It's three gray beanies that have the word *Buddies* on them.

"Oh my gosh, those are cute!" Tatum gushes.

"They aren't the same size, though. These two are way too small. Unless one is meant for you?" I suggest, then hand it to her, but she shakes her head.

"Won't fit me either."

"Huh, okay." I set them down, then look for the third one.

I unwrap a small wooden music box. As soon as I open it, a lullaby plays.

"That's precious," Tatum says softly.

It is, but what a strange thing to give a man. "Yeah."

Next, I open a white stuffed bear with a little red heart on its tummy. "I'm starting to wonder if she was drunk when she put this together."

Tatum giggles. "I think there's a theme."

"Well, there's only one left, so I guess I better figure it out." I pull it out and unwrap some material. Holding it up, I stare at a heather gray shirt.

"Oh my gosh," Tatum gasps, and I realize there's something on the other side. I flip it over and read it.

HUN-CLE: Like a normal uncle but way more good looking

"Wait..." I smirk, grabbing the second envelope like Piper demanded. Inside is a sonogram photo with small white text written on it. *Hi, Uncle Easton! There are two of us!*

"No way. Look!" I hand it to Tatum, and the wide smile she wore earlier drops.

"That's amazing. Congrats," she says softly.

"So damn exciting, don't ya think?"

"Mm-hmm. Do you still want me to record?"

"Nah, I'll call them right now!" I look at the camera. "Very sneaky, you two!"

Tatum ends the video, then hands my phone back to me so I can FaceTime them. I click on Piper's name, and her face appears almost immediately.

"Did you open it?" she squeals.

"Yeah, you're getting puppies, and I'm gonna be a dog-uncle! Double trouble!"

Tristan chuckles in the back as Piper glares at me. "My babies aren't dogs, you jerk!"

"Oh c'mon, I'm just messing with you. I'm so happy for you guys! About time. I've been waiting to teach kids how to surf!"

"Yes, that's exactly why I got pregnant," she deadpans.

"Do you know their genders yet?" I ask.

"Girls!" Piper responds immediately.

"You can't keep telling people that," Tristan scolds, then looks at me. "We don't know yet."

"My instincts say they're girls, and they're never wrong," Piper declares. "Two sweet little angels that I'll get to put in cute pink dresses."

"Oh hell no, you're not dressing my nieces like pageant queens."

Piper narrows her eyes, then takes a piece of chocolate from an almost empty Dove bag.

"Excuse me, I'm the one pushing them out, so I will do whatever I want," she demands.

I chuckle, knowing that's true. Piper has always danced to her own beat.

We chat and laugh for a few more minutes, and when I look over at Tatum, she's quiet and lost in her head. She chimed in to say hello and to congratulate them but hasn't engaged further.

"Alright, I'm gonna let you two go. Thanks for the fun package. I'm gonna wear that shirt proudly. Even on their wedding days."

Tristan snorts. "If they're even half as high maintenance as their mother, they won't allow that."

"Hey!" Piper squeals. "That's not fair. No one would want their uncle to wear a T-shirt talking about how handsome he is on their wedding day."

"Okay, I'll compromise. Just to the reception."

Piper chuckles. "Let's discuss it in thirty years, okay?"

"Alright, deal."

Before we say our goodbyes, Piper reminds me to send her the recording. As soon as we hang up, I text it to them both.

Tatum's demeanor is off, and I can't pinpoint what happened to upset her.

"Everything okay?" I ask, shifting closer to her.

She smiles, but it looks forced. "Absolutely! That's really exciting for them."

"Yeah, considering my brother isn't getting any younger and Piper probably wants a dozen babies, they were bound to start having kids as soon as possible. Twins will keep them busy as fuck, though."

"She's lucky. I struggled to get pregnant. It can mentally fuck you up as a woman."

Wait, what?

"You did? I had no idea, Tatum. Was there nothing that could be done to help you?"

"I should rephrase that. I could *get* pregnant, but I struggled to keep the pregnancies. I miscarried. Over and over. It was frustrating and mentally exhausting."

My heart squeezes at how sad she is right now. I can't even imagine what that was like or how it made her feel. "I'm so sorry."

"I wasn't trying to make this about me. I'm sorry. It's just a trigger that still haunts me."

I grab her hand. "Don't apologize. I'll never understand how it felt to go through losses like that, but it doesn't mean you have to hold back. I can sympathize with how painful that must've been," I tell her, not knowing much about pregnancy or babies but seeing the anguish written on her beautiful face.

"About ten years ago, I made it to the second trimester. I was so damn happy and followed the pregnancy books to a T. I was twenty-five weeks along when I lost him. They called it a stillbirth. I was devastated, and it was one of the darkest times of my life."

I shake my head. "Do they know why?"

"No. It's rare, but it happens more often than most people realize. That was the first time Justin hit me."

I blink. "What? He hit you after something so tragic happened?"

I must be hearing her wrong because what kind of *man* does this to his wife after losing a baby?

"He was upset and took out his anger on me. Of course, he apologized, but it was the start of my emotional spiral."

I grind my teeth, shocked and pissed that Tatum went through a horrific experience with a shitty fucking partner.

"We stopped communicating. Instead of grieving together, he used me as a punching bag to relieve his stress, and the support I needed wasn't there. I was too ashamed to tell anyone because I thought he'd snap out of it. Then I blamed myself. If only I hadn't lost the baby, we'd be happy. If only I was a woman who could handle pregnancy, we'd have a family."

I want to bash that motherfucker's face in the concrete.

"You're strong, Tatum. You went through something unimaginable and came out ahead."

She scoffs. "I'm not sure that's true."

I brush the hair off her face, then tilt up her chin to look at me. "It might not matter anymore, but in the event it does, you can open up to me about anything. Cry in my arms. Let it all out. Whatever you need, okay?" I give her a reassuring smile. "You deserved better. You shouldn't have had to deal with that mental warfare."

"I think it would've been different if I'd had a support system, but I was already isolated from my friends and family. I hadn't noticed it at first, but then Justin told me I wasn't allowed to tell anyone. As if he was *embarrassed* I couldn't carry full-term. Truthfully, I should've gone to counseling for my grief, but he refused to pay for it. Instead, I was expected to just pick up where I was before we lost him like nothing had happened."

"He's a piece of shit, Tatum. You have no idea what I'd like to do to him."

She wipes her cheeks after a couple of tears fall. "Trust me, a few horrible thoughts have crossed my mind, and I don't even want to tell you what Oakley says about him. It took a few years after that to realize he was a narcissist. So many ups and downs, controlling and manipulative behaviors, and me being naïve by thinking he'd eventually change."

I want to hold her tight right now.

"But Easton, I'm sorry to be a Debby Downer. I don't want

to take away from your amazing news. I'm really excited for you and your family."

"I'm not upset, Tatum. I mean, *I am*, but not about that. I wish I could've been there for you, that's all."

She nods, choking back more tears. "Thank you. I need to freshen up. I'll be back in a bit."

"Take your time. I'll be here." I shoot her a wink, and she blushes.

"I appreciate everything you do for me. Whoever you end up marrying one day will be one lucky woman."

CHAPTER TEN

TATUM

DAY 13

I WAKE up with a heaviness on my heart. I hated the way I reacted yesterday during Piper's twin pregnancy announcement, but it brought back way too many painful memories. A future I should've had but was stolen from me. When I think about my loss, there's an emptiness rooted deep inside. Sometimes, I wonder what my life would be like if the pregnancies had gone full-term. If I'd have a loving husband and a house filled with happy children, or if Justin would've still been a controlling asshole. All I can do is push the thoughts away because none of that happened, and it's not the reality I get to live.

When I was a little girl, I didn't dream of a big wedding or a huge house. I imagined having kids of my own. It's all I ever wanted. A few tears spill down my cheeks, and I hurry to push them away. There's too much sadness, hurt, and anger, and I try to forget what happened time and again, though I know those memories will live with me forever.

Once I'm settled and free from Justin again, I'm going to

search for a therapist in the area. Someone who deals with miscarriages, grief, and manipulative exes who weaponized my losses. I know I need help. I haven't been away from him long enough to be able to fully heal, and just when things were looking up, Justin came back to remind me that he's always been in control and still is.

He disgusts me.

After I've cried some more in the bathroom, I splash water on my face, then try to gain control. Once I've calmed down, I go downstairs, where Easton is sipping a cup of coffee. I make a mug and sit next to him. He meets my eyes, and I know he knows I've been crying but doesn't mention it.

"What do you want to do today? It's your turn to decide. The world is your oyster," he says.

"Hmm." I tap my index finger against my lip. "There's one thing that I've been wanting to do ever since I was a little girl."

Easton tilts his head at me. "Guess it's time to make your dreams come true."

I laugh. "I didn't tell you what it was yet! I could say skydiving or bungee jumping."

"I'm game. Don't even have to think twice about it."

"This is why I enjoy spending time with you. There's something about an adventurous man…"

A brow pops up. "Yeah? You find that hot?"

I snort. "It's a good characteristic to have."

He's grinning. "So what is it? You want to find grizzly bears? Go to Greenland? Climb Mt. Everest?"

"Collect seashells."

His smile softens. "That's *it*? Guess today's your lucky day. The tide is going out soon, and that's the best time to go hunting."

"Really? I didn't know there was a schedule for this."

He finishes his cup. "Yeah, high tide brings in the best

shells, so you go look around when it's low. After a storm is the absolute best!"

"How do you know all this?" I finish my last sip and grab a yogurt from the fridge.

"Every Easter, we'd celebrate by finding eggs and hunting for seashells. It was a nice memory. Mom loved collecting them. Next time we're in the garage, I'll have to show you the ones we've saved over the years."

"That sounds amazing. I would've been in heaven."

Easton checks the time on his phone. "Go change, and let's go before it gets too hot. I'll grab the sunscreen. Don't want a repeat of last time."

I chuckle, excited as I finish eating. Once I'm done, I rush upstairs to change into the bikini Easton got me and slip on some cutoffs. Before I walk out, I take a quick glance at myself in the mirror, then throw my hair up into a high ponytail.

He's waiting for me with two sand pails in his hands. "This one's for you, milady."

"Appreciate it," I say, and we make our way to the beach. The sun hangs lazy on the horizon, and I can never get enough of this view.

Easton walks close beside me as we make our way to the shore. There are a few runners out, which is typical in the mornings, but for the most part, the beach is deserted.

"Sunscreen," he reminds, then squirts some in my hand. I cover my arms and stomach, then grab the bottle so I can do my legs.

"Want help with your back?" he asks.

I smile. "That would be awesome."

Easton rubs the lotion in his palms to warm it up, then massages it into my skin. He takes his time, making sure he touches every inch, and I can't help the heat that rushes through me. As he kneads my shoulders, my breath hitches, and I'm thankful he can't see my face.

When Easton speaks up, his voice is thick and gravelly. "You're tense."

"I could use a good massage," I admit, but it comes out in a hoarse whisper. I love his strong hands on me and how my body reacts to him, but it also scares the shit out of me. It's been a long time since I've felt anything like this before, regardless of this being innocent.

When he pulls away, I immediately feel the loss. I turn, meet his eyes, and see something swirling behind his gaze.

"You need some help too?" I ask, wanting to return the favor.

"Yeah." He hands over the bottle. Then I take my time touching him. His muscles flex, and I can't help but admire how they cascade down his back. Freckles sprinkle across his shoulders, and I'm tempted to trace them with my fingers. I'm breathless, trying to calm my racing heart as he lets out a hum.

Does he feel the same things I do? Or is it all in my imagination?

When I pull away, Easton turns, and our eyes lock. He swallows hard, clears his throat, then thanks me.

"No problem," I say, trying to find my words. He puts the sunscreen in his bucket and leads me closer to the water.

"This is where you have to look," he says, bending down and picking up a shell that's long and twisted.

"Wow, this one's neat." I study its texture. "I'm so excited."

I let the wet sand squish between my toes, and when I look back, I can see our footprints in the sand. We're quiet as we collect beautiful shells in different shapes and sizes. I try to be selective with the ones I take because I'm too tempted to pick up every single one I see.

"Check this out," he says. Walking closer to me, he's holding something that's lime green.

He places it in the palm of my hand, grinning wide.

"Oh, what is this?" I turn it around and hold it up in the sunlight, where it nearly glows.

"It's sea glass. You can find different colors, and people collect it like crazy. I'll have to show you some of the amazing art made from it."

"So this is *actual* glass?"

Easton nods. "Yep, from broken bottles that have been weathered. It's smooth around the edges, almost like a rock."

"Yeah, wow. I guess I never realized this was a thing."

"A lot of jewelry makers use it." He's standing close, almost too close, but I don't want him to pull away.

"Is it rare?"

A chuckle escapes him, almost as if he's nervous that we're standing so close. There are too many unspoken words swirling around us. I dig my toes in the sand, unwilling to create space even though I should.

"Depends on the color. Oh look," he says, pointing at another piece on the ground.

I pick it up, and it's an amber color.

"Sometimes, when the sun hits it at the right angle, it reflects the light. That's a nice one."

Holding my palm open, he scoops it into his hand, then lifts it up to the sky. Seeing him find joy in something that I've always wanted to do makes me happy. Of course, I'm still wound up and anxious, but Easton makes it easy to forget all the bad.

He hands it back, and I place it in my bucket. We make small talk for the next hour, and I take the opportunity to learn more about him.

"When did you know that you loved surfing?" I ask, curious.

"Oh, that's easy. The first time I got on a board. There's something about catching a wave and using your body to maneuver across the water. People say magic doesn't exist, but anytime I surf, I can't help but think it does."

"That's amazing. It's a great hobby."

"So is yoga," he finally admits. "Even if I'm terrible at it."

"It's fun. Keeps me busy and focused on other things. Plus, it keeps me flexible. Other than that, I don't have much going for me. At least not like you."

He tilts his head, meeting my eyes. I like it when he looks at me with that intense fire behind his gaze. "I might own a business, but what else do I have? It seems great, but sometimes, it's lonely too because most people don't understand that sort of responsibility. At least not anyone my age."

"I get that," I say.

"I don't have someone to share any of this with. No one to spoil or celebrate with." He slows his pace. "Family's great, and I love my job, but I can't help feeling like something major is missing in my life."

I open my mouth and close it, trying to come up with the proper response as the waves crash beside him.

"When the right person comes along, you'll know. Being with someone, getting married, and doing that whole thing is overrated when you rush into something. Waiting to find *the one* is worth it." I try to lighten the mood and shoot him a wink. "Coming from personal experience and all. I mean, I'm no relationship pro or anything."

Easton gives me a side smile. His shoulders relax, and we continue walking. Our arms brush together, and I like being this close.

"I've been thinking about something," I admit. "You asked me recently why I stayed with my ex for so long."

"Yeah," he says with a soft tone. This time, I stop and turn to him.

"It's a question I've been asking myself for a while, and yesterday, when I was meditating, I realized the answer."

He waits for me to continue.

I swallow hard, feeling the knot form in my throat. "I couldn't give him a family, and I felt broken. In a way, I believe that if I gave him the babies we dreamed of having, it would fix our problems. That I owed it to him to keep trying, to stay with him, to fit the mold of the doting wife regardless if I was nearly swallowed whole by my depression. I knew there were deeper problems, but I ignored them and blamed myself. It was easier." A few tears spill down my cheek, and Easton sets down his bucket and wraps his arms around me. As he holds me tight, I give myself permission to let it out because I kept it inside for so long.

With him holding me like I'll slip through his fingers if he lets go, I feel safe.

"You don't owe *anyone* anything, Tatum," Easton whispers. "You're enough just as you are."

Sobs escape me because no one has ever said anything to me like that and meant it. "I'm a failure."

He pulls away and wipes away my tears. "You're not. You're strong. Beautiful. Caring. And it destroys me that you can't see that. Your ex was lucky to have someone like you, who stayed and was willing to sacrifice their own happiness. But that's not how it's supposed to work, sweetheart."

"I was brainwashed into believing everything was my fault. Then one day, I woke up. It's like the blinders were removed, and I saw how toxic his persona was. Leaving was the only choice. More like escaping. If he'd known what I was planning, he'd have killed me before I tried and blamed it on my depression. Then I saw the signs outside of your shop about the job and apartment, and my entire life changed."

Easton smirks. "For the better, I hope?"

"Absolutely. I think sometimes people come into your life for a reason. I have no idea why, but I wouldn't have been able to navigate on my own without you. I was handed the freedom I desperately craved because I could never go back to Nebraska. For the first time in my life, I did what I wanted. It was exhilarating but frightening."

"Life is strange like that sometimes, and things just work out. I'm glad I met you, Tatum." He smiles.

"Me too," I admit, and we go back to seashell hunting. I find more glass, and when we decide to head back because we're both starving, my eyes widen.

"Oh my God!" I yell, bending over to pick up a fully intact sand dollar.

Easton runs over. "Holy shit! This is incredible."

"I've always wanted to find one of these but didn't think it'd ever happen."

"It's rare to find them not broken. When we were kids, we called them mermaid coins."

"Really? That's kinda adorable," I admit, ecstatic.

"Yeah, it's actually really lucky. They say they're a good omen and a sign for good things to come."

I look down at the sand dollar in my palm and am overwhelmed with happiness. It holds way too much meaning for me, and I'd be lying if I said it didn't give me a sliver of hope.

Easton gives me a high five, then we head toward the house. Maybe, just maybe things will get better. I hold the sand dollar tight, hoping and praying it will.

CHAPTER ELEVEN

EASTON

DAY 14

AFTER A DAY of taking and making calls, I feel mentally drained. Apparently, the investigation into what happened to my shop is still ongoing, but I'm hoping to hear something back next week. While I don't want them to rush their review, I'm growing impatient.

Tatum has been such a huge help, and we were able to get the inventory sheets together and submit them. There was more in the shop than I realized, and all I want is for everything to be the way it was before so I can try to recoup some money from the shop being closed. It was the absolute worst timing, but it usually is when disaster strikes.

After I take a shower, I change clothes and meet Tatum in the kitchen, where she's cooking something that smells amazing. I move toward the stove, and she looks over at me with a smile.

"Wow, whatcha making?"

"Thought we could do some shrimp tacos and black beans. I even made homemade tortillas."

My eyes widen. "We had the ingredients for that?"

She chuckles. "Yep, and they turned out perfect."

My mouth immediately waters when I see the guacamole she made. "I'm so relieved you know how to cook. Honestly, if I were here alone, I'd be living off tuna and Spam."

She pretends to throw up in her mouth. "Spam? Disgusting."

"Hey! It's not so bad when you put it in a skillet and heat it up."

Tatum holds up her hand to stop me from saying more. "The smell is enough to make me barf. Canned meat is a big no for me."

"It's a bachelor's specialty. Ooh, you know what goes good with tacos?"

She shrugs.

"Mojitos."

"Not sure I've had one before."

My jaw drops. "What? Never? Okay, we're going to change that right now." I go to the liquor cabinet Piper had stocked and pull out the ingredients. Considering I grew up in a beach town, this drink is always paired with seafood. I have the recipe memorized.

I set the rum, mint syrup, and lime juice on the counter, then grab some glasses and fill them with ice. After I pour the perfect drink, I give it a stir, then hand it to Tatum to sip.

"It's missing one ingredient," I admit.

"What's that?"

"A mint leaf," I tell her.

She snorts. "That sounded so pretentious."

"I try," I say with brows raised as she takes a sip.

"Okay, I think I'm in love," she blurts out. "With a mojito," she corrects.

"Not a bad thing to be in love with." I make mine in the

other glass. Once she's made her tacos and added cheese, I grab everything and set it on the table.

Once it's all laid out, I observe her brushing loose strands of hair from her face.

"You could be a chef. Look at this."

"I've always loved to cook, but Justin loved the same meals, so I never got to experiment."

My face softens. "I love to eat, and I'm always down for trying anything you want to feed me. Otherwise, it's Spam and cheese sandwiches."

"Don't mention that again. The visual has my stomach roiling." She gags, and we sit.

I grab a few tacos, and she opens the chips.

"I read a funny surfing joke today," Tatum says.

"Really?" I ask around a mouthful. "Tell me."

"Okay, it's corny, but I chuckled." She takes a sip of her drink. "Why do surfers eat cold food?"

I shake my head, waiting for her answer.

"Because they hate microwaves."

I nearly choke on a shrimp and clear my throat.

"Holy shit, are you okay?" she asks with worry in her eyes.

"Yes," I say, sucking in air. "That one caught me by surprise, but it's hilarious."

She grins. "I was looking up surfing facts, and I saw that one on a forum. I usually suck at telling jokes, so I'm glad I didn't ruin the punchline."

"I think it did the job."

She chews on her bottom lip. "Good thing I know how to do the Heimlich maneuver, thanks to my sister."

"Oh yeah?" I ask, loving how she's sharing so much about herself. Though we've been here for a while, I feel like she's just started to share little things about herself she may have never shared without the fire. Guess I can be grateful that it brought us closer together, even if spending time together won't last forever.

"One of Oakley's friends nearly choked at a party. They didn't know what to do, so she forced me to take a class with her. I didn't want to go, but it's a good skill to have. You never know when you'll need to save someone's life."

"Do you know how to do CPR too?"

She nods. "Everyone should know those things just in case you need to use them."

I pop a chip with chunky guacamole in my mouth, then notice Tatum finished her drink.

"Want another?"

"Absolutely. Keep 'em coming. I really like them!" Tatum says as I scoop up her glass. I chug mine and make us another round.

I return to the table with our fresh drinks and sit. "Be careful. They'll sneak up on you."

"Perfect. It's been a while since I've had a buzz. Actually, I can't remember the last time."

"Then I'll go heavy on the rum for the next one."

She snickers. "I won't complain."

I finish my tacos, then snatch up another. Tatum does too. When we're finished eating, I offer to clean up the mess and put everything away.

"Ooh, refill time," I announce, quickly making and bringing her another. I barely feel anything, but I can tell Tatum is growing tipsy. She lifts it to her lips and chugs it down, then hands me the glass.

All I can do is laugh, but when I return, I hand her some water with her drink. "Don't want you to feel like shit tomorrow."

"That's thoughtful. Thank you."

I plop down in front of her. "So now that we've had dinner and drinks, what do you wanna do."

Tatum looks at me with hooded eyes, and my cock springs to life. I have to remind myself that she's my employee and not ready for any kind of relationship. I've always been intrigued by her, and I can never get her off my mind, even when she's sitting right in front of me.

"What about a game?" she offers. "Any suggestions?"

I go to the game closet and start reading off the titles.

"Instead of choosing any board games, let's play two truths and a lie. When I was in high school, it was always a fun one," she says.

Grabbing the bottle of rum from the counter, I walk back to the table and sit directly in front of her. "You sure?"

"Why not?" She shrugs, and I actually kinda like this free-spirited version of Tatum.

"Who goes first?" I ask.

"You can. Just remember one of them has to be a lie, and I have to guess which one it is." Tatum lifts her glass to her lips and drinks.

"Those are the rules, and I'm sticking to them." It takes me a minute to think of something, but I eventually do. "I've never broken a bone. I've had a threesome. I never learned to write in cursive."

Tatum stares at me as I give her my answers. "Hmm. Now that's a hard one. But I'm gonna guess the threesome."

I chuckle. "That's true."

Her eyes widen, and her jaw drops as if she really didn't think that'd be the correct one. "No way! When?"

"During my early twenties. These two best friends I met at a bar were fighting over me, so instead of making me choose, they decided to share. It was…an *experience*."

"Wow…that's wild."

"Definitely was…but I'm a guy, and I wasn't about to turn down the offer." I chuckle.

"Did it happen more than once?"

"Yeah, went on for a couple of months until I realized that it'd never go anywhere. So I ended it. Then I met my girlfriend Brynne less than a year later, and we dated until I opened the shop four years ago."

"Well, regardless, I bet that was a fun experience for you. Two women at once. That's a guy's wet dream." She picks up her drink and gulps the rest of it down.

I shrug. "I suppose. After a while, it's exhausting, and you kinda feel used. Not all that it's cut out to be. Plus, the jealousy between the two friends never ended. More trouble than benefit, if you ask me."

"So what was the lie?"

"No broken bones. However, I broke my arm when I was eight. Rollerblading accident. Your turn. Bet you can't fool me."

She lets out a steady breath and stares intently at me. "Cocky, aren't you?"

"Maybe a little." I smirk.

She clears her throat. "I've never had an orgasm during sex. My favorite food is sushi. I can whistle really loud."

"Easy," I scoff. "Orgasming during sex."

Tatum slowly shakes her head.

"What? How is that possible?"

She shrugs. "It just never happened for me."

"It's because you haven't been with the right partners," I explain. "Sometimes, it's really about the motion in the ocean."

Tatum bursts into laughter.

"So you like sushi?" I ask.

"I love it," she admits. "And I can't whistle for shit."

"Damn, this game is going to be much harder than I thought."

"You're telling me," she says, taking the top off the rum and gulping down a shot.

"Guess it's my turn again, then. Hmm." It takes me a minute to think about what I'm going to say next.

"Scared?" She arches a brow.

"No." I chuckle. "One of my biggest fears is being bit by a snake. I've never had a roommate. I used to be a vegetarian."

"Vegetarian? That's the lie."

"Absolute truth," I counter.

"Really? Why the change of heart?"

"I go through different phases. I watched this horrible documentary and gave it all up. I love animals and try to limit my intake but realized it wasn't sustainable for me long term."

"Wow. Takes a lot of courage to admit that. So is the lie snakes?"

"Yep. My *biggest* fear is losing a family member, especially my brother. He was in the military and had a close call, and I just remember being in such a dark place, thinking he wasn't going to make it. Of course, he did, and he's happy now. He's basically my best friend, and I'd do anything for him."

"I'm sure the feeling is mutual."

"Oh it absolutely is." I think back to the conversation Tristan and I had the other day. I know my brother cares about me just as much.

Her face softens. "I'd do anything for my sister as well. Since she's so much younger, I am very protective of her. I just don't want her to go through the same things I did when it comes to being in a relationship. But then again, she didn't stay with the first man who told her he loved her, so I think she's in the clear."

"And all that is in your past now. Time for you to start thinking about the future and what you want to do."

Tatum grins. "You're absolutely right."

"Have you thought about any of it?"

She chews on the edge of her lip, and I find it adorable. "A little. I'm hoping all of this blows over with Justin, and I can enjoy being in Florida without constantly looking over my shoulder. I want to move on, and I hope one day I really can, but with that being said, guess it's my turn again."

The alcohol is starting to affect me, and I know Tatum's feeling it too.

She thanks me, then begins. "New Year's Eve is my favorite holiday. I've never been on a real date. I could eat an apple every day and never get tired of it."

I narrow my eyes at her, hoping the date one isn't the truth. "This is tricky."

She chuckles. "That's the point."

"I don't think you could eat an apple every day. That sounds fishy."

She snorts. "You're right."

But then my heart breaks for her. It's as if she notices my demeanor change, and she avoids my gaze.

"You know you're going to have to explain," I tell her.

"I know. It's weird to say things like that out loud because they should be lies. Justin never tried because he didn't have to. We'd been together since we were in high school, so going on dates just didn't happen."

I look at her in disbelief. "That's not an excuse. My parents have been married for decades, and they still go on dates."

"See, I still make excuses for him, even after all this time. Pathetic."

I reach across the table and place my hand on top of hers. "No. That's just what you truly believed. He didn't see what he had in front of him and didn't appreciate your love. That's not your fault that he didn't try or care to do things with you like that. It's on him."

"Thank you," she whispers. "I think for so long I just accepted the way things were because he destroyed my self-esteem. I didn't feel like I deserved any of those things. He'd make underhanded comments about the way I looked or what I was wearing. After several miscarriages, I started believing everything he said."

"I'm sorry," I tell her. "I'm sorry he was such a piece of shit to you."

She nods. "Me too."

"I just hate that you can't see what I see, Tatum."

Her eyes shift up and meet mine. "What do you see?"

"A beautiful, caring woman with a fighting spirit who's in the process of finding exactly who she is."

"Meeting you might have been one of the luckiest days of my life."

My face cracks into a smile. "I feel the same."

CHAPTER TWELVE

TATUM

DAY 15

I HONESTLY CAN'T BELIEVE I've been here for two weeks. Sometimes, it feels like only yesterday when we were escaping the shop, and other times, it feels like a lifetime ago. I've learned so much about Easton and have shared a lot about myself in the process. He's easy to talk to, and I find that I'm able to be real around him. The more I open up, the easier it is to be myself.

As I wipe down the counter after making an afternoon cup of tea, I hear my phone buzzing. When I grab it off the table, I see it's my lawyer calling.

"Hi, Tatum," he greets.

"Hey, what's up?" I've learned that when he calls, it's usually for a reason.

"I just wanted to let you know that your ex-husband will be meeting with his lawyer and me next week. You're not required to be present, and the conversation will be recorded, but I wanted to make sure you haven't changed your mind about anything before I go there."

I clear my throat, which feels like it's slowly closing. "I just want a divorce. He can have whatever he wants."

"You're entitled to half of everything," he reminds me as I mix a tablespoon of honey into my cup.

"The quicker I can put this behind me, the better. I want nothing from him other than a clean break."

He lets out a sigh. "I understand. I just wanted to confirm before I speak with the two of them."

"Thank you."

"Mr. Nichols seems very eager to have this resolved. He seems like he's finally ready to sign the paperwork and move on. His lawyer was extremely adamant about meeting next week, and I actually had to cancel an appointment to fit them in."

My jaw clenches, and my entire body tenses because I don't trust this. I've been hoping for months he'd move on, sign the divorce papers, and let me go. And all of a sudden he wants to conveniently get it over with? Why? What's his real motive?

"So he'll be there? In person?"

"Yes," Wallace confirms, and I have no reason not to believe my lawyer. "I assume he's leaving Florida. Maybe the temporary restraining order made him realize there won't be a resolution."

"I could only hope," I mutter.

Wallace tells me to reach out if I have any questions and that he'll keep me updated. When I end the call, I'm frozen in place with my phone gripped in my hand.

"Everything okay?" Easton asks, and I nearly jump out of my skin.

"Shit. You scared me."

He chuckles. "Sorry. You have this look on your face."

"It was Wallace. He said Justin will be there next week to

sign and finalize the divorce." I pick up my tea and take a few big gulps now that it's cooled some.

Easton's smile is contagious. "That's amazing news, but you don't look happy."

"Something is going on. I'm glad he'll be going back to Nebraska because the restraining order only lasts two weeks. I'm just apprehensive because Justin knows how to manipulate and control me, even from afar. This could be one giant plan to trick me or—"

"Tatum. If I've learned anything over the past decade, it's not to worry about things you can't control. Otherwise, you get so caught up in it that it consumes you. When my brother was injured, I drove myself mad wondering if he was going to die. Finally, I told myself to take it one day at a time, that it was something I couldn't control, and there was nothing I could do besides support him. So for now, let's assume it's legit but stay guarded and prepared in the event it's not."

I release a breath and nod. "You're right. I just think about how close I am to really being free and starting over. Things in my past haven't typically worked out in my favor, so I guess I'm jaded in a sense. Jaded to being happy because the rug has been pulled out from under me too many times to even get excited anymore."

His brows furrow. "That makes me sad."

I take the opportunity to drink more tea. "I know, but I can't help it. Justin has made me this way. I'm always on the defense waiting for the next punch because I feel like one is always coming."

"One day, you'll look back at this and realize how much you've grown and how strong you are to have made it to the other side of this craziness."

"I hope you're right."

He takes a step closer. "It's a bet I'd be willing to make."

"Not one I'd take. I may not get excited about the future or believe good things happen, but I can't bet against myself. That would be ridiculous."

"Because you know it's true."

My face cracks into a smile. "It is."

"Eventually, the clouds will move away, and you'll be able to see blue skies. This situation you're in isn't forever. It's just for right now. And next week, once those papers are signed and processed, you'll be able to start fresh."

"That's the dream. And honestly, I am happy that Justin will be meeting with them because that means he won't be here." I look down and see Easton's holding his laptop. "Going to do some work?"

"Yeah, I thought I'd catch up on some emails. I know the adjuster needed me to send something over, and I've been trying to place orders with my vendors to be delivered in a few months."

I meet his eyes. "When the shop is rebuilt, it's going to be crazy trying to get everything set up and running again."

"I know, but..." He taps his temple. "I'm not worrying about the future. Just the things I can control right now."

I laugh. "Yeah, yeah. I just think it's in my DNA to worry, but I'm going to try to do better. When I find myself stressed, I'm going to focus on my breathing. I honestly didn't realize I was doing that until about five minutes ago when you pointed it out. It's almost like you notice things that I don't. I'm not used to having someone care about me."

His eyes soften again. "I care about you more than you know. I'm here for you, and I've been told that I'm a good listener, though I am a smart-ass sometimes."

"Thank you, Easton. I appreciate that."

He plops down on the couch and opens his screen. I finish my tea and rinse out the mug.

"I think I'm going to soak up some rays. Get in some yoga and meditation," I admit, feeling the tension in my neck.

"I'll be watching from here," he teases.

I go upstairs to change into some leggings and a tank top. Considering it's the end of June, it's hot as hell outside, but I love it so much.

After I'm dressed, I grab a towel and my iPad, then head outside. Feeling the warm breeze against my skin and hearing the distant waves crash in the ocean is like having my own oasis. Being here with Easton really is like a paradise. One I didn't know I needed until now.

I stretch first, then open an app that goes through different yoga poses with calming music. It has a countdown that makes it easy to follow.

I picked a thirty-minute workout, which didn't sound like a lot, but my muscles burned just halfway through. Basic yoga was too easy. Intermediate had me sweating, but today, I chose advanced. Not sure what I was thinking. My limbs are like spaghetti noodles by the time I'm done. But I'm more relaxed than I was when I started.

Afterward, I turn on a guided meditation video and get lost in my breathing. Each time my mind wanders, the instructor pulls me back to my center. I try to stay focused and follow the instructions. When it ends with a namaste, I lie back on the towel and watch the fluffy clouds slowly drift overhead. The conversation I had with Easton repeats in my head, and I don't know what I did in my past life to deserve someone like him.

There have been times when I've wanted to cross the line, where my body has begged to feel his strong, warm hands, but I've resisted. Am I even ready to be in a relationship? The last thing I need is a rebound or another messy breakup.

"There I go," I mutter to myself, worrying about things for

no reason. I suck in a deep breath and slowly let it out, regaining control of my thoughts again. Somehow, they drift back to Easton and those green eyes that pierce straight through me. I don't know how it's possible for him to know me so well in such little time. But I appreciate it in ways that I could never fully explain to him. I think he knows that, though.

After a couple of hours outside, I decide to go in.

"How was it?" Easton asks.

"Great. I feel a million times better," I admit. "But now I smell. I think I'm gonna take a bath."

"Okay, enjoy yourself."

I look at the clock and see it's just past six. I take my iPad and prop it up on the counter to watch a movie. After I add some honey bubble bath, I undress and slide inside. A laugh escapes me as Adam Sandler talks about nudie magazine day in *Billy Madison*.

I'm so relaxed that I nearly fall asleep. Eventually, the water turns lukewarm, and my fingers prune. Though the credits haven't started running yet, I know I'm at the end of the movie, which means I've been in here for over an hour.

Once I'm out, I throw my hair into a high bun and put on a sundress. My stomach growls, and I realize I haven't eaten since lunch. As I go downstairs, I realize the lights are dimmed, and there are lit candles on the table. Next to the white plates are cloth napkins and silverware.

My mouth drops when I see Easton leaning against the counter, dressed in a button-up and slacks. He flashes me that boyish grin that always makes my body hot.

"What's going on?" I ask, looking around at everything.

He takes a few steps forward, and I can't help the way my eyes wander down his clothes. I honestly never thought any man was perfect until him. "Thought we'd have a date night.

The way you always deserved to experience. I wanted to give you one since you haven't."

"Wow...really?"

He walks over to the table and pulls out one of the chairs for me to sit. My nerves begin to get the best of me, but I don't know why. We're friends. We've known each other for months. I should feel comfortable, but this seems real, like there's something deeper behind it.

"I wanted to do something special for you." He picks up a small remote, and soft music plays on the surround sound. Easton goes to the kitchen and pulls out a pan of lasagna. He carries it to the table and puts a hefty portion on each of our plates. "Don't worry, I made dessert too."

I chuckle. "I wasn't upstairs that long. How did you manage to pull all of this off?"

"Planning makes perfect," he admits, sitting down in front of me. The flames dance, casting shadows on his face, and I love the way he's looking at me.

"If I'd have known, I would've dressed up," I say, feeling completely out of place.

"You look beautiful, Tatum. I think you're dressed perfectly."

"Thank you," I admit, heat meeting my cheeks. I'm glad the lights are dim so he can't see how much he affects me.

I pick up my fork and cut into the steaming lasagna. "I can't believe you cooked something as gorgeous as this. It's perfect."

"What if I told you the meat inside is Spam?"

I set my fork down, and Easton bursts into a hearty laugh.

"It's not," he says. "I promise. But the look on your face? Priceless."

I meet his eyes, not fully believing him.

"I swear," he offers, blowing on a bite before he pops it in his mouth.

I follow his lead, and my eyes widen when I taste the amazing flavors. "This is…incredible."

"It's my mother's recipe. When I was younger, it was a tradition we had together. I learned how to make the noodles from scratch. Brought back a lot of good memories when I was preparing them tonight."

"I can't believe this is homemade."

"I actually made the dough yesterday and hid it in a drawer. I was worried you'd find it and ask what it was. Glad you didn't, though. I love surprising you."

I want to inhale the plate in front of me but take my time, enjoying Easton's company.

"Will you teach me one day?" I press the napkins to my lips.

"Absolutely. It's a process, but one that's worth it."

"It's so good." I chuckle.

"What?" he asks, taking a sip of his wine.

"I just can't believe you cooked this. Maybe you've been holding out on me this entire time, and you're secretly a chef."

He coughs and shakes his head. "This is about the only thing I can make. Though, I feel like I could probably follow a recipe."

"We all start somewhere," I tease. "But this is phenomenal. Paired with the wine. I don't deserve this."

"Yes, you do," he declares. "This and more, and if I have to spend the next six months proving that to you, I will."

"Is that a promise?"

"You bet your ass," he taunts.

I chuckle, taking my garlic bread and scooping up the remaining sauce from my plate.

"Want more?" Easton asks. "There's plenty."

"Oh gosh no. It was the perfect amount. Any more and you'd have to carry me upstairs."

His brow pops up, and he smirks. "That can be arranged."

I snort. "I dunno if you can carry me."

"Are you kidding me? You're as light as a feather."

"I'm heavier than I look," I confirm.

"We'll have to put that theory to the test. You know I like a good challenge." He grins.

After Easton puts up the food, he sets several expensive-looking bottles of wine on the bar. Glasses are waiting for us along with more candles. I appreciate how much care and planning went into making tonight special.

"I thought we could do a wine tasting," he offers. "Piper had the place stocked before she was pregnant and told us to drink it so she wouldn't be tempted when they came to visit."

He sets several bottles in front of me, then sits right beside me at the bar top. "I can't even pronounce some of these names." I don't even try.

"That's a 2003 bottle of Egon Muller Scharzhofberger Riesling Trockenbeerenauslese," he reads, slightly butchering it with a horrible accent.

"Sounds like a mouthful."

He lifts a brow and meets my eyes with his heated gaze. Then he quickly clears his throat. "Apparently, this vineyard is located in Germany, and it's the best Riesling on the market. Have you had it before?"

I shake my head. "No, before tonight, the only wine I ever had was with a screw top."

He chuckles. "Another first then." He pours a small amount in the bottom of my glass and then does the same for his. Then he raises it, and I lift mine too.

"A toast to you. Here's to many firsts. I can't wait to experience more with you."

Heat rushes through my body, and I chew on my lip. "I'd like that," I honestly say.

The tension in the room grows thick, and right now, I want nothing more than to slide my lips against Easton's. By the way he's looking at me, I think he wants the same, but I'm not sure. I don't know what to look for because I've never really had to date anyone. We gulp down the wine, and my eyes widen. It's the most delicious thing I've ever had, and I can't believe it's alcoholic.

"Did you like it?"

"Are you kidding? It was amazing."

"You should totally download the wine tasting app on your iPad and add these to your list. Riesling is sweet. Light and well-balanced. And don't let the color fool you. It will totally fuck you up because it's easy to drink fast."

My head falls back with laughter. "Noted."

The sweet, light flavor is still on my palate, and I want more. "You only gave me one tiny sip!" I push my glass toward him. "Fill it halfway."

He tilts his head and holds his hand out to show all the other wines we'll be drinking tonight. "We still have six more bottles to open, but I won't argue. It's great." He refills both of our glasses with triple the amount of his first pour.

Easton pulls out his phone and adds the wine to his app. "Get in close, and hold your glass. I want to add a picture to the entry."

His warm body presses against mine, and he lifts his phone. I smile, noticing my face is already flushed. After he snaps it, Easton shows me.

"It's perfect," I mutter with a grin.

"Yeah, it is."

"Can you text it to me?" I ask.

"Sure thing. I can actually AirDrop it to your iPad."

"Oh okay, awesome."

I quickly grab my tablet and set it down next to his phone. He presses a button, and the picture is delivered immediately. It opens up on the big screen, and I smile at how happy we look. If anyone else saw this, they'd easily assume we were a couple. I lock the iPad and set it to the side, though I feel like I could stare at that picture all night long. This is a memory I'll never forget—I'm thirty-seven and experiencing my first date.

I gulp down the half glass of Riesling and enjoy how smooth it is. "I taste peaches and something else."

"Apricot," he confirms. "It's very citrusy but finishes nicely."

"Totally. So what do we have next?" I turn to look at him as his arm brushes against mine.

His voice is deep and raspy. "You choose."

"That one." I point at a clear bottle with liquid the color of tea.

"Nice choice. We have a Disznoko Eszencia Tokaj." He hands me the bottle to look at, and I didn't expect it to be so heavy.

"Originated from where?"

"Hungary, I think." Easton uncorks it and adds some to our glasses. He swirls his around and smells it, then I follow his lead.

"Wow, this smells amazing." I swallow it down, and I nearly gasp at how delicious it is. "Holy shit."

He chuckles. "I know. What would you say it tastes like?"

"A hint of caramel and honey. I can't quite place it, but it's really good. Very rich. I can see why it's considered a dessert wine." I swirl the liquid in my glass, then gulp the rest down. I can feel the alcohol moving through my system, and my entire body feels like it's on fire. Not sure if it's Easton and the way he looks at me like I'm the most beautiful person in the world or the wine. Either way, I'm not complaining because it feels good to be with him like this without a worry in the world.

"Oh, I almost forgot…" He stands and walks to the fridge, then pulls out a tray. When he comes back, he removes the lid from a plate of chocolate-covered strawberries. "The chocolate really makes it taste different. Take a bite."

Easton holds the strawberry in his hand for me, and I lean in, meeting his eyes as I bite down on it. Juice runs down my chin. He grabs a napkin and wipes it off as I finish chewing.

"Now take a sip," he instructs, and I can see the fire behind his eyes. I do exactly what he says, and the flavors are explosive. I close my eyes and let out a moan, enjoying the taste of the dark chocolate mixed with the sweet undertones of the wine.

When my eyes flutter open, Easton is staring at me, the strawberry still in his hand. He swallows hard, then quickly changes the subject. "How about we open one more?"

"That would be great because right now, I want more of these two."

He chuckles and pushes forward a bottle that looks like it came off a pirate ship. "How old is this?"

"It's an 1812 J. S. Terrantez Madeira from Portugal," he says. "Piper said it had a different taste, but it was good in its own way."

"You're telling me this bottle of wine is over two hundred years old? Is that safe to drink?"

He snorts. "You're cute."

"I won't be if this wine gives me the shits," I blurt out.

A roar of laughter escapes him. "Wine can last a long time. But if that happens, we'll suffer together."

Easton pours us each some, and I smell it like I did previously, then take a small sip. "Okay, that's delicious."

"I'm actually surprised too," he admits. "It's got a floral taste."

"Yeah, it's hard to place it. There's something else too. Clove?"

He nods in agreement. "Yeah, and maybe apricots."

"It's weird but strangely good. I'll have another one of those," I say, plucking a strawberry from the platter. Easton rejoins me at the bar, and he turns his body toward me.

"Which was your favorite?" He lines the bottles up next to one another.

I tap my finger on my lips and reposition myself to face him. Electricity bolts through me when I meet his gaze.

"I'd say the first one. I like how light and sweet it is. It's not too heavy like the second one or strange like the third one."

He nods, agreeing. "Same. How much do you think it cost?"

"You said Piper bought these, right?"

"Yep." He grabs the Riesling and nearly fills our glasses.

"Five hundred dollars?"

As he takes a sip, his eyes are glued to mine. He shakes his head. I hear the unspoken words and wonder if he's actually reading my mind right now. Sure, the conversation is moving forward, but I can't concentrate on anything but him.

"More?" I ask, his knees brushing against mine.

"Much, much more," he says, snatching a strawberry.

"I have no idea. Probably a thousand." I drink more of it, knowing it wasn't cheap, and knowing I wouldn't have gotten this experience any other way. I could barely afford new clothes, and simple luxuries like this weren't ever in our budget when I was married.

"Twenty thousand," he says, and I nearly choke.

"Oh my God, Easton. We're drinking something that cost more than the first car I bought. You're kidding, right?"

"Nope. The second one is fifteen hundred, and the third one costs a little over thirteen grand."

"That's too much. I feel terrible. I don't deserve this."

Easton grabs my hands. "You're worth it. Piper actually suggested we open these."

I sigh. "Then I guess we better drink every last drop, considering we opened nearly thirty-five thousand dollars' worth of wine."

"As I mentioned before, her love language is buying expensive things for people because money doesn't matter to her. If it makes other people happy, that's what she wants. My brother found a good one."

I suck in a deep breath. "I'm just not used to anyone being so generous. Or as kind to me as you have been. Did you tell her that you were planning a date night?"

He chuckles, his breath brushing against my cheeks because we're sitting so close. "No. She texted me and told me to help myself to all the wine. I thought this would be the perfect occasion to crack it open."

"Thank you." I can't help the wide smile that spreads across my lips, and I hear Elton John's "Something About the Way You Look Tonight."

"Want to dance?" Easton asks.

I stumble as I stand, but he catches me in his arms and laughs.

"You good?" he asks.

"Yeah, great." I smile.

He takes my hand and leads me to the living room, where we dance barefoot. Gently, I place my hands behind his neck, and his firm grip grabs my hips. We sway to the music, and I get lost in the moment with him holding me close. I don't want this moment to ever end. An intense sensation rushes over me as I think about the night and where it's led us.

Easton spins me around just as Eric Clapton's "Wonderful Tonight" starts. Emotions bubble to the surface, and I find myself smiling. Happiness like this is something I've missed, but I know it won't last. He sings along, and I feel his grip tightening on me.

Falling for my younger boss was never a part of the plan, but I can't deny the way I feel deep inside. I've gotten the impression he's attracted to me and would be interested in something more than friendship, but given my situation, he's held back. The same reason I've been holding back too. But at this moment, it's like none of that messy stuff matters.

As the song ends, Easton pulls away with a lust-filled smile. I look up into his green eyes as my heart races, and my breathing becomes ragged. He has me under his spell, and I can't pull away. Slowly, Easton leans in, and my eyes flutter closed as I anticipate his next move. When his soft lips press against mine, I'm floating into unknown territory. Our tongues twist together, and I fist his shirt. One of his hands threads through my hair, and I moan against his mouth.

"Tatum," he says as I devour him. Our bodies are so close that I can feel his hard cock pressing into me. I feel a need and desire I haven't felt in so long that my heart races with anticipation.

A few steps, and I could push him onto the couch. I imagine straddling and riding him.

"Fuck," he groans, and knowing how turned on he is encourages me to keep going. I want to. I need to. But I also know we have to stop. It's the responsible thing to do.

Though it pains me to do so, I pull away and meet his gaze. "I'm sorry," I whisper.

"No, no," he cuts me off, but I think he also realizes we've crossed the line.

My lips are swollen, and though I want more of him, I

don't want to make it awkward. Especially since we're kinda stuck together for a while longer.

"I should go to bed," I tell him and study his face.

"Okay. Let me clean everything up, and I'll walk you upstairs," he offers.

"I appreciate it, but I'm fine." I give him a smile, wishing I knew what he was thinking. I force a yawn. "I'm gonna pass out as soon as my head hits the pillow."

He chuckles, but I know there's something more he wants to say. "Sweet dreams, Tatum."

"Thank you for the perfect night. It's something I won't ever forget."

Easton smirks. "Maybe we can do it again sometime?"

"I'd like that," I admit, my heart fluttering as I walk away from the only man who's sparked something inside me. I really did drink a lot, but I was in complete control of my actions. Easton was too, or he wouldn't have let me walk away. We both know we were lost in the moment, even if we both wanted it.

When I walk into my room, I slip off my dress and look at myself in the mirror. My lips are swollen, and my face is flushed. My hair is a little messy from where he tangled his fingers in it. Just the thought of him consuming every inch of me is enough to drive me crazy.

I lie down on the bed and slip off my panties, then get comfortable under the blankets. Sliding a hand between my thighs, I rub small circles over my clit. My pussy throbs as I imagine Easton's fingers on me, touching, licking, and devouring every inch. The fantasy overtakes my mind as the sensation builds inside me.

Soft moans escape, and I can't remember the last time I had an orgasm. My body begs for the release as I slowly slide one finger inside. It's not enough, so I insert another, then press my free hand over my mouth as guttural groans ring out.

Heat rushes through me as I return to my hard bud. My breasts rise and fall as I teeter on the edge.

"Mm…Easton," I whimper, wishing he could hear me moan his name. I imagine the way he'd fuck me raw and break me in all the right ways. I know he'd be an amazing lover just by how attentive he is with the most basic things.

As I imagine his tongue flicking against my clit, the orgasm rips through me. My muscles tighten, and as I spill over, my body convulses into rapid shakes. It takes every bit of strength I have not to scream out. When I finally come down from my high, I realize how sweaty and worked up I am. Easton's gotten under my skin in the best way possible, and there's nothing I can do about it. As scared as I am to admit it, I think I've slowly fallen in love with him.

CHAPTER THIRTEEN

EASTON

DAY 16

THE SUN BEAMS through the windows, and I look at the clock on the bedside table and see it's just after seven in the morning. Last night in bed, I couldn't stop thinking about Tatum and how she felt so right pressed against me. She leaned into me, twisted our tongues together, and for a moment, I thought she was going to give us what we both wanted. As soon as she said she should go to bed, I knew kissing was as much as she could handle right now.

The electricity I felt as our mouths connected is something I've never experienced before.

Knowing there's no way I'm falling back to sleep, I climb out of bed and say good morning to George. He scurries around his cage, and I wiggle my finger between the bars before giving him a treat.

Afterward, I walk down the hall and see Tatum's door is cracked. When I peek inside, she's still asleep. Her golden-brown hair is splashed across the pillow, and if I weren't so chickenshit or concerned how she'd react, I'd climb under the blankets and hold her to my chest. Then I'd tell her how goddamn beautiful she is. Instead, I go take a cold shower.

Standing under the stream, I close my eyes and replay last night in my head. Tatum kissing me and fisting my shirt in desperation. She wanted me, and fuck, I'd be a liar if I said I wasn't ready to carry her to my bed.

I roughly grab my erection and stroke it as fantasies play out in my mind. I imagine her perky nipples in my mouth and licking down her stomach to her wet pussy. I grip harder, placing my other hand against the wall and steadying myself. My breathing grows more ragged until my balls tighten. It doesn't take long before the orgasm rips through me, and I release a groan of pleasure.

A few seconds later, a knock taps on the door.

"Yeah?" I call out, trying to calm my erratic heartbeat.

"You alright?" Tatum asks from the other side.

"Fuck," I whisper, not realizing how loud I was.

"I'm fine," I tell her, trying to keep my voice steady.

"I thought I heard you yell something. You sure you're fine?"

I can think of a million ways of how she could help me, and we could start with her perfectly plump lips around my cock. "I'm good, but thank you for checking on me."

"No problem. I'm going downstairs."

"I'll meet you in a few minutes," I respond, grabbing the bar of soap and washing my body. After my dick has settled and I've rinsed off, I grab a towel and dry off. Once I'm good to go, I wrap it around my waist and head to my room.

"Shit," I say, remembering my jeans are in the dryer. Since I only have a limited amount of clothes, I've been having to do laundry every couple of days. I go downstairs, and as soon as my foot hits the hardwood, Tatum looks up at me from the table. She's holding her cell phone out, so I assume she's FaceTiming her sister.

"Yeah," she says, and I can hear Oakley chatting about something.

Tatum's gaze slides down my chest to my stomach, and then she studies the imprint of my cock, before meeting my eyes again. I arch a brow and smirk, but keep my thoughts to myself. As I walk away, I can feel her eyes on me. I slip on some jeans and a T-shirt.

When I return, she ends the call and focuses on her iPad. I make an espresso and sit in front of her. She swallows hard as she watches me. There's something behind her gaze—want and desire. If I didn't know better, I'd say she's two seconds away from devouring me whole.

I clear my throat. "How did you sleep last night?"

She hesitates for a second as a touch of blush hits her cheeks. "Great. Once I crawled under the blankets and settled in, I was out."

I picture her upstairs, lying naked under the sheets, and think about how soft her skin would feel against mine. I'd do anything to feel her soft skin and worship her the way she deserves. "That's good."

After I take a sip of my coffee, I offer to make her breakfast. Tatum sets down her iPad, and I hold up a hand before she can argue.

"Let me. It's hard to fuck up avocado toast with an egg. Even for me," I reassure her.

"But not impossible," she rebuttals. "That would be great, though. Thank you."

I go to the kitchen and quickly prepare everything, then set the plates down on the table. Tatum grabs forks and napkins, then we sit. We make small talk, both of us ignoring the fact that our tongues were in each other's mouths last night.

Pretending that we didn't want to bring this to the next level when it was more than obvious we did. Skirting around the elephant in the room becomes more difficult when the attraction is so damn undeniable.

Tatum laughs. "My sister was in a mood today."

"Oh yeah? How so?" I ask. As she talks, I can't help but notice how the sunlight reflects off her hair. Her complexion is smooth and perfect, and I love the way her lips tilt up when she says something amusing. When I look into her crystal blue eyes, I feel as if I'm lost at sea and never want to be found. Selfishly, I don't give two shits when my apartment gets rebuilt because it means I get to spend more alone time with Tatum. Without her here, I'd probably be going crazy and be bored off my ass, but now I'm dreading the day we leave. Eventually, we'll have to get back to our regular schedule, but I hope I have enough time to crack open her hard exterior before that happens.

"You know what I mean?" she asks, taking a bite of avocado toast with an egg on top.

"Yeah, definitely." I was so lost in my thoughts staring at her that I wasn't listening. She doesn't notice, though, because her gaze stayed locked on mine the entire time.

After we're done eating, I clean up and meet her back at the table. She's fully invested in something on the screen.

"Whatcha reading?" I ask, noticing she swipes through book pages.

"*How to Get Away with Murder*," she states flatly.

I tilt my head at her and narrow my eyes. "Should I be hearing this? I don't want to have to testify against you."

Tatum snorts. "Nah. It's just a self-help book."

My brows shoot up.

"Kidding! I'm reading a romance book that sounded interesting."

"Really? So you're reading porn?"

She smirks. "I mean, some books are heavy on the sex scenes, but some focus more on the plot and characters. Just depends on the book, I guess. Though lately, I've been in the mood for spicy novellas. They're quick reads with lots of hot scenes, and honestly, I'm a little jealous."

My cock hardens at hearing her talk about this. I clear my throat again and adjust myself in my chair. "Hmm. Like what kinds of scenes?" All I'm picturing is the porn I used to watch where the pool boy gets seduced by the older woman whose husband was never home.

"There was this one where the hero and heroine did it against a wall. In a pool. In the back of a car. Basically, every surface they could find. But I can't help feeling a little envious of how lucky this girl is. The way she explains it makes me think I've missed out on quite a lot."

I palm my cock to tame it down. Now is not the time to get a boner.

"Maybe you should add it to your sex bucket list then," I suggest. "Places to have sex before you die."

She chews on the edge of her lip as if she's making a mental note. "If you could do it anywhere, where would it be?" she asks.

"Hmm, that's a hard one." I scratch my cheek, thinking hard about it. "I've always wanted to join the mile-high club and do it on an airplane."

Tatum chuckles. "The bathrooms are so tiny, though. Makes me wonder how many times you'd smack your head."

"That's part of the allure. I like being adventurous, though."

"One of my fantasies is oddly having sex in a public place," Tatum admits, her cheeks burning bloodred. "Just the

THE HEART OF US

anticipation that you could get caught seems sexy and dangerous."

She sucks in her lips, and I'm certain she squeezes her legs together. I don't miss the way her nipples stand at attention. The fact that she's not wearing a bra right now, and I can see through her white shirt is sexy as hell. Almost as if she *wants* me to notice.

"Voyeurism. There's an entire kink for it."

"Have you ever done it?" she asks nervously.

"No, but I would with the right woman."

I see her heartbeat throbbing in her neck and wonder what she's thinking.

"Maybe I should make a list for when I'm ready to start dating again. Though, the thought of putting myself out there is kinda frightening," Tatum admits. "There are too many damn apps and expectations. I feel like it'd turn me off from men more than wanting to find a good one."

That makes me laugh. "There are. It's probably why I've stayed single for so long. I always hear that you'll meet the right person when you're not looking. So I haven't been looking…for *years*. Most who have shown an interest are too immature and just want to party all the time. I just can't relate."

"I don't even know what I could relate to, honestly. What are men my age doing? Because the ones I knew back home had country club memberships and cheated on their wives after golfing all Saturday. And if that's the case, I'd rather stay single. Plus, I think most people on those dating apps sign up to have random hookups only. I might not have a ton of experience with only having one relationship and all, but I know that one-night stands aren't for me."

I meet her eyes, and guilt rushes through me. Does she assume that's all I'd want her for? Is that why she pulled away last night before things could escalate? Still, I'm too damn chickenshit to bring it up because I don't want to make her uncomfortable or be awkward around me.

"For me, going out with someone just for sex isn't worth it. I realized that I need a deep connection with someone first for it to be genuine. I'd rather save that for the woman I'll spend the rest of my life with."

"I'm sure you'll find someone who's perfect for you, Easton. You have a lot to offer someone. Too bad we didn't meet in high school," she says with a laugh. "I bet you were fun to be around."

"When I was starting high school, you would've been twenty-three. Totally illegal, but I still would've been on board." I chuckle, and she does too. Given the story I shared with her about my English teacher, she knows all too well my preferences on older women.

I wish I could put my heart out on the table right now, but I can't. My fear of rejection or making Tatum feel out of place holds me back once again.

"You have a lot to offer someone too, Tatum," I tell her, wishing she could see what I see in her.

She scoffs. "No. I really don't. But maybe one day I will."

Tatum sets her iPad down on the table.

"Another place I'd love to have sex somewhere in public is Germany. Maybe in a big park."

"Damn, that's a risky place," I say hoarsely. "Everyone would be able to see and hear you."

"That's the point, but it would be in a different country with little to no risk of someone recognizing me there."

"Isn't it illegal? I know in some European countries it is."

"It's not. Road sex is legal in The Netherlands. That'd be another fun adventure to try."

Is she trying to fucking kill me? The casual way she's

talking about public sex makes me wonder if she's just trying to rile me up or get some kind of reaction. The only reaction I have at the moment is how much my dick likes hearing her talk about sex. I reach under the table and adjust myself once again. At this point, there's no way she hasn't noticed.

"Oh, that's quite interesting," I croak out. I'm in desperate need for a subject change.

"I'd like to do it in the back of a car too," she states, not getting the memo that I'm dying inside. "Never done that, but it's shown in movies and books so much, I wanna experience it myself. Maybe some off-road sex under the stars."

"Roads? Where we're going, we don't need roads!" I exclaim.

Her brows furrow, and she squishes her face. "Huh?"

"*Back to the Future*," I explain in shock that she doesn't recognize the infamous line from Doc Brown.

Tatum shakes her head. "Never seen it."

My mouth nearly falls to the floor. "It's literally a classic. What do you mean you've never seen it? You pick on me for not seeing a nineties movie, but this one's from the eighties!"

She shrugs. "Just haven't. There are actually a lot of movies I've never seen."

I stand. "That changes tonight."

"We're going to have a movie night?"

"Sure are. We can finish the wine we opened last night and make popcorn after dinner."

A wide smile spreads across her perfect lips. "I'm excited. First, date night and now, a movie night. Are you trying to court me?" she says in a light teasing voice, but I hear a hint of something else.

"I could ask you the same thing. You're the one who keeps entertaining these wild ideas of mine. You are starting to give me the impression you're waiting for a marriage proposal soon. Perhaps you should just tell me your ring size now."

She snort-laughs and shakes her head at me.

Tatum's phone vibrates. "It's Oakley again."

"Have fun," I say, then go upstairs and grab my laptop. When I'm back in the living room, I open it up and get updates on different things going on with the shop.

For the rest of the day, Tatum and I go our separate ways, and after we eat a quick dinner, she cleans the kitchen. I set up the surround sound for the movie and make a bowl of popcorn. Once I set the bottles of wine on the coffee table, I grab us two glasses. Then I dim the lights.

Tatum joins me and sits as close to me as she can. For the first thirty minutes, I stare intently at the TV, but I can't seem to focus on anything but how her smooth skin feels against mine. I'm drawn to hers in ways I can't explain, and right now, I want nothing more than to feel her lips on mine.

I pour us some wine, and we both take a sip, agreeing how good it tastes. When we set them down, our eyes meet, and I swear hers are begging for me to kiss her again. Before I can talk myself out of it, I cup her face and gently press my lips against hers. I take it slow, giving her the opportunity to pull away if she wants, but she doesn't.

She melts into me as I run my fingers through her hair. She responds by grabbing my bottom lip between her teeth and tugs, then sucks on it. I'm so goddamn hard that my cock feels like it's going to break off inside my jeans.

Tatum moans against me, and seconds later, she's pushing me down on the couch. I let her take full control of the situation as she straddles me. Of course, she's wearing a dress again, so I catch a glimpse of her red lace panties. Her head falls back on her shoulders as she grinds against my erection. Tatum falls forward, her lips capturing mine, and I squeeze her ass, wishing I could slip a finger inside to see how damn wet she is.

"Fuck, Easton." She groans loudly as she rocks against me.

"What do you want, Tatum? Tell me what you need," I beg, wanting her permission to do all the dirty things I've been dreaming of and more.

"I don't know." She breathes out, flustered and worked up. I love seeing her this way.

Reaching up, I slide the strap of her dress down and pinch her hard nipple. Then I move to the other and massage it in my palm.

"Your tits are amazing," I tell her, desperate to take them in my mouth.

I want every single inch of this woman, and by the way she's getting off rubbing on me, I think she wants that too. Her movements grow slow, ragged, and I wonder if she's close.

"Yes, sweetheart," I murmur, giving her full permission to take what she needs. Her body is begging for release. I can see the desperation written all over her face of how badly she needs it. She slides her hands down and unbuttons my jeans. I swallow hard and meet her eyes. Then she dips back down, and her mouth crashes to mine.

Frantic and hungry, I love seeing Tatum so damn greedy for what she wants, and I'm willing to give her everything she needs.

CHAPTER FOURTEEN

TATUM

I DON'T HAVE control of myself right now, but it feels so good to be with Easton like this. The more I rub my clit against his jeans, the more buildup it creates. If I continue at this rate, I'll come just from the friction alone.

Taking full control, I reach down to unbutton his jeans. I massage my tongue with his, but it's not enough. I need more of him. As he palms my breasts, I rock my hips faster.

The little voice in my head tells me this is a bad idea and that I should stop, but I can't find the strength to pull away. Just one move and Easton would be inside me, filling me with his thick cock. I've caught glimpses of it when he's been hard, and I already know he'd destroy me. Something I fantasize about happening.

"Fuck, baby. You feel so good." Easton moans as he lifts his hips to meet me. "God, you're so beautiful, Tatum."

His words nearly knock me back to reality, and I abruptly pull away.

"Everything okay?" He brushes the hair out of my face and studies me as I hover above him.

THE HEART OF US

My panties are undoubtedly soaked. I swallow hard at how embarrassed I am that I basically just mauled him.

"You're the only man I've been with who's ever told me that." For some reason, my emotions start to bubble as I realize what we're doing. "I don't know why, but it caught me off guard. I'm sorry."

Carefully, I climb off Easton's lap, my body immediately feeling the loss of him. I adjust myself as Easton tucks himself back into his jeans.

He's just as flustered as I am.

"No apologies. Come talk to me," he urges, patting the couch and taking my hand. It's a kind, friendly gesture, one I appreciate.

"I just...I dunno. This is all confusing for me. I'm fighting a war inside my head right now and when you called me beautiful, it's such a foreign term of endearment to me that I immediately felt unworthy of the word."

He rubs his thumb across mine. "I'm never, ever going to apologize for telling you how beautiful I think you are. You deserve to be told that every day of your life."

"Compliments are hard for me to take. They always came with conditions."

"Emotional abuse," he states, and I'm so sick of hearing that term. It immediately makes me out to be a victim. Even if I am, I don't want to be labeled. I also don't want what Justin did to me to affect this new chapter of my life.

"Yes, very much so," I confirm. "I warned you about me. Flawed in many ways, damaged, uncertain. You deserve better than that."

His expression softens as he presses a gentle kiss on my knuckles. "You're beautiful. You're smart. You're caring. You're fun to be around. You're an amazing cook."

My face cracks into a shy smile.

"You're patient. Your laughter is literally contagious. If those are considered flaws, then yes, you're full of them."

I snort at his cocky remark.

"All that, and somehow, you wonder why I like hanging out with you."

"Insecure, unstable, a mental disaster even on my good days," I counter. "There's a lot I still need to work on."

"I don't believe that about you, but even if you were, that doesn't make you any less of a worthy person. I hope you know that," Easton states matter-of-factly. "I find everything about you desirable."

His words are too much, and I'm not quite sure how to respond. He thinks so much of me, and I'm not used to that. Easton has a literal front row seat to my flaws and everything else that I'm going through, and it's like no matter what, it doesn't scare him off. He's too damn perfect to be real.

"Want some more popcorn?" he asks, pausing the movie that we've now missed the past ten minutes of.

"Sure," I tell him, and he squeezes my knee before going to the kitchen. One thing I adore about him is the way he makes me feel comfortable even in embarrassing moments. He respects my boundaries even when I'm the one who oversteps them.

On the one hand, I want Easton more than I want water on a hot summer day. On the other, he's too young, and I'm too broken. I know he needs someone who can give him everything he wants in life. I want to hand him my heart, and I know Easton's the type of guy who'd meticulously try to glue it back together. I've never felt such a strong pull of emotions about a man before, but he's my exception.

Easton returns with more popcorn, and thirty minutes later, the movie ends. I missed a lot of it, but I tell him I enjoyed it. Which for the parts I did see, is true.

He looks at the clock, and it's barely past eight. "Guess we can watch *Back to the Future 2*."

I chuckle. "Right now?"

"Yeah, I mean, if you can handle such a great movie."

I playfully roll my eyes. "I guess we'll see."

Easton presses play, and as soon as the movie begins, I notice they changed the actress who played Jennifer and gasp.

"What the hell? Why didn't they use the same girl as Jennifer?"

"I know," he says, pausing it. "People were ready to burn the freakin' world down when this one was released, but it was a sad story as to why."

"What happened?"

"Claudia Wells' mother was her manager and was dying of stage four cancer at the time. So instead of accepting the role, she gave up acting for a little while to be at home with her."

"Wow," I say, feeling horrible for being pissed.

"Crazy, huh? It worked out though, because spoiler alert, she returned twenty-six years later to do the short film they released in 2015."

"Wow, that's cool."

He laughs. "Yep. This is why this series is such a classic. Michael J. Fox is a national treasure."

"No kidding. He accomplished so much."

Easton unpauses the movie, and I watch while being glued to his side. He grabs a blanket and covers us as I lean my head on his shoulder. I don't know what we're doing right now—basically snuggling like a couple in love—and it feels like we're stuck in a weird limbo.

Easton would've let me do whatever I wanted. That much was clear. Losing control with him was never my intention, but he didn't seem disappointed when I stopped. I'm confused as hell, and the last thing I want to do is give him mixed signals. I don't even know what it is that I should do, even if I know that it's him I want.

Easton begins to yawn, and so do I. Mentally, I feel like I'm a wreck and am actually looking forward to staring at the ceiling for the next hour to try to unpack what happened tonight.

Once the movie is over and everything gets turned off, Easton walks me upstairs and stops outside my bedroom door.

"Good night, beautiful." He leans forward and places a soft, lingering kiss on my forehead. "Sweet dreams."

Butterflies swarm my stomach so fast, I nearly pass out at the sensation.

"I'll never stop telling you that." He winks, and all I want to do is press my lips against his and have him carry me to his bed.

"Thank you," I whisper. "Night."

I somehow break away and go into my room. I lean against the door, trying to calm my rapidly beating heart. At times like this, I don't know what to do and wish someone could give me the right answer. I got so caught up in letting Justin control my every move that I tend to flounder when it comes to decision-making.

And then I think, what if I screw things up with Easton and the only man who's ever had my back? Losing him as a friend and boss would be devastating.

Sucking in a deep breath, I grab my phone and call my sister. She's the only person I can talk to about situations like this.

"Hey, sis," she picks up with a laugh. I put her on speakerphone, and it sounds like she's at a bar or restaurant.

"Am I interrupting something?" I ask. "I can call back if so."

"Nah, just picking up some food before I head back to my apartment. Didn't realize I'd get to chat with you twice today. It always makes me happy to hear your voice."

"I guess I just miss you," I say sincerely. "But I didn't want to bother you either if you were busy."

"I'm not. What's up?" she asks. "There's an edge in your voice that makes me think something's on your mind. Spill the beans, sis."

I release a breath and sit on the edge of my bed. "I feel like a naïve teenager who's falling for someone she shouldn't be falling for."

"I freaking knew it!" she exclaims. "Glad you're ready to finally admit what I've been saying for months."

I huff. "I just don't know how to process what I'm feeling. I'm confused and can't stop thinking about him. All this stuff with Justin and my low self-esteem…I just feel like he can do better than me and that I'd hold him back in life. I'd be the dead weight. We'd be like Megan Fox and Machine Gun Kelly. Everyone would wonder why the hell he was with me."

"Oh my God…" I hear a door open, then close. "First off, I'm partly proud you know pop culture references. However, you're wrong."

"Well, we wouldn't be no Ryan Reynolds and Blake Lively."

"To be fair, no one can live up to them. They're the royal family of America."

I snort, although I'm having an internal crisis. Oakley has a way of making me laugh even during the times I want to cry.

"Tell me this. Is he flirting with you back? Or is it one-sided? Be honest!"

"Well…" I linger, thinking about all the times he's hinted about relationships, has told me how beautiful I am, or how he winks at me. I mean, if that's not flirting, then the guy has boundary issues..

"It's mutual. I didn't want to see the signs at first, but they've become more apparent the longer we've been here. And even before then, he had little flirty comments that I never took to heart, but perhaps I should've. Truthfully, I'm not sure how long I've ignored the signs, but they're impossible to ignore now."

"Then you shouldn't be hung up. Easton sounds like a really smart guy and would know what he'd be getting into if he got into a relationship with you."

"We've kissed," I whisper.

"What did you say? I didn't hear you."

"Yes, you did," I snap, playfully rolling my eyes. "More than once. And tonight, I was ready to strip him naked but stopped midway. I got in my head too much. I know he's my boss. And he's nine years younger than me. He's closer to your age than mine."

"Age doesn't matter once you're out of high school, Tate. No one cares about that, except maybe you. If Easton's pursuing you, why don't you just give him a chance and see where it goes?"

"Because what if it doesn't work out? I don't think I can handle another failed relationship right now."

"Okay, but what if it does?" she retorts. "What if he's the love of your life, and you push him away and right into another woman's arms?"

Just the image of that makes me want to stab someone.

"I'm scared to fall in love again, Oakley. Scared I'll get hurt or that my heart can't love again. Scared I'll be the one to hurt him. Scared for many reasons, honestly. But with that being said, these feelings I have for him can't be ignored for much longer. It's rooted deep, and the more I try to ignore it, the harder it becomes to be around him. I want to lose myself with him. I want to so damn bad, but I'm so hesitant to cross those lines."

"You've said time and again how he's a good, decent guy. He's done more for you than Justin ever has. Plus, he seems to always have your best interest in mind."

"He does," I agree. "I hate that I keep comparing him to my ex, though. I wish I could permanently block him out of my brain."

"Go a few rounds with Easton, and I'm sure he'll push him out of there."

I burst out laughing. "Of course you'd say that."

"Well, you're the one who keeps saying he's hot as hell," she adds.

I snort. "I did have an immediate attraction to him from the day we met. But I mean, who wouldn't? Easton is sex on legs. Those green eyes, dark hair, big muscles. You should see him surf. He's the perfect man and deserves a woman who's perfect just like him. I can't be that. I'm Sandra Bullock in *Miss Congeniality* when she tries walking in heels for the first time and falls flat on her face. That's me."

"Really impressing me with these references, Tate." She giggles. "But ya know what? Maybe you're perfect to him? Just because your versions of perfect look a certain way doesn't mean his are the same. Justin was a fucking asshole and tried to destroy your psyche. Not all men are like that. From what you've told me about Easton, he's not like that either." I can hear someone call her name, and she says something back to them. When she's in her car, she continues. "You're a catch, sis. Don't let your fears hold you back from something that could potentially make you really happy for the first time in years."

I swallow hard, fully taking in her words and knowing

she's probably right, but I still have my doubts. "He has his whole life ahead of him and—"

"And deserves someone who he wants to spend the rest of his life with, right? That could be you, but you have to take the chance. Let's say it doesn't work out. What do you lose?"

"A friend. A job. A place to live. *Everything*."

"You really think Easton would fire you or kick you out if you two dated and it didn't work out? I doubt he's that heartless."

"No, but it'd be awkward as hell. I wouldn't want to be the ex who is still in their lives and sees them every day, especially if feelings were still involved. I don't know if I could handle him being with another woman after he was with me. I'd probably feel some jealous rage," I admit, which even takes me by surprise.

"Spoken like a woman who knows what and who she wants."

"I do want him. So much." I whimper, then fall back on the bed and watch the ceiling fan go round and round.

"Give him a chance then. Give *yourself* a chance to be happy again. The last thing you want me to do is fly to Florida to kick your ass, so stop being so damn stubborn. Come on. You're smarter than this, but maybe your little sister needs to come shake some sense into you."

I chuckle, knowing she probably would. "You're right."

"As I usually am," she sasses. "Sometimes, you have to take risks to reap the rewards. I just have a good feeling about this. Honestly, I can't wait to be the maid of honor in your wedding."

"Oh now you have me marrying him?"

"Yep, that's right. And I can't wait to tell you I told you so."

"Yeah, yeah," I tell her. "We'll see about that. Not sure I'll ever get married again, though."

"I guess I can understand that, but your name would sound so cute as *Mrs. Easton Belvedere*," she sing-songs, and I cackle at her dramatics. "Just promise me you'll think about what I said."

I smile. "I promise. And thank you."

"For what?" I hear her car start.

"For being the best damn sister in the world. I don't know what I'd do without you."

"Probably be depressed. I mean, I'd be because I'm pretty badass," she states confidently.

"I pray for the guy you end up with. I hope he has lots of patience and can deal with your sass."

"I'd be offended, but you're not wrong. Men my age are annoying and lame, so I'll probably end up with an older man. And I probably haven't met him yet because he's still with his first wife, who's been secretly having an affair with his brother."

"What in the Wattpad have you been reading?"

"How do you know about Wattpad?" She gasps, and I chuckle.

"I'm not a prude!" I retort. "You make me out to be a nun sometimes."

"Ha! Now go let that hunk of a man rip off your nun habit and get to your fun parts."

"Good Lord. I'm leaving now. Text me when you make it home so I know you're safe. Love you."

"Love you too. Now go have tons of sex," she blurts out before I end the call.

My mouth hurts from smiling so much. Oakley always puts me in a good mood. However, maybe she's right. Maybe Easton and I would have a fighting chance if I gave us a shot.

Perhaps, it's time to find out.

CHAPTER FIFTEEN
EASTON

DAY 17

TATUM'S CALL with Oakley echoed into the hall. I wasn't trying to eavesdrop, but I couldn't walk away once my name was mentioned. Call me a nosy bastard, but I wanted to hear Tatum's responses.

And she confirmed everything I thought.

She wants me as much as I want her, and I fully understand her hesitations and concerns. I have them too. But I know what's in my heart, and I'd regret not giving us a chance until the day I died.

Tatum has no problem fooling around, but then she gets lost in her head with doubt. My plan is to do whatever I can to change that.

Falling asleep didn't come easy since I was consumed by thoughts of her, which meant I ended up sleeping in. By the time I make it downstairs, it's almost noon.

"Good afternoon, sleepyhead," she teases from the sofa with George's cage on the coffee table in front of her. She's sitting in a cute sundress with her legs tucked and the iPad against her knees. "I was getting worried."

"Yeah, I know. I haven't slept this late since I was a teenager. Guess my body needed it." I go to the kitchen and make a cup of coffee.

Tatum comes over, and I immediately smell the scent of her shampoo. She looks up at me but seems nervous.

"I've been reading this book all morning, and there was a specific scene that inspired me. I want to try something if you'll let me."

I arch a brow, then set my mug on the counter. "Okay."

"Alright, I need you to stand very still. Don't move."

"Uhh...sure," I say as she grips my arms and holds me steady.

She inches closer. "Wait. I'm too short. Hold on, I need to find a step stool."

"No need." I grab the back of her thighs and scoop her up, then set her butt down on the counter.

She squeals, holding me. "I guess this works too."

I stand between her legs as they hang off the edge. She swallows hard, realizing how close we are. "Now, put your arms behind your back and close your eyes."

I do as she says, anticipating her next move.

She's silent for several seconds. All I hear is her heavy breathing until her palms gently cup my face. I know she can feel how fast my pulse is beating, but I can tell hers is too.

Finally, she presses her lips to mine. She carefully brushes her tongue along my bottom lip before pulling away.

"You aren't kissing me back," she says quietly.

Keeping my eyes shut, I remind her, "You told me not to move."

She releases a groan. "Maybe this was a bad idea."

Oh hell no. Her fear of rejection is overpowering her ability to be honest.

"Tell me what you want, Tatum."

"I-I don't know."

I open my eyes and tilt up her chin. "You're in control here. Whatever you want, I'll give you. Remove all your doubts and insecurities, and listen to your heart. What do you want? I'll never do anything without your permission."

"I want you to kiss me back," she states.

"I thought you'd never ask."

She leans in, cautiously colliding her mouth to mine, and as soon as her tongue slides between my lips, I deepen our connection. I palm her cheeks but let her lead the pace. She pulls me closer, wrapping her thighs around my waist and pressing my body against hers.

My mouth slides down her jawline, and she releases a moan as I suck on her earlobe. When her head falls back, I drag my teeth along her skin.

"You're so damn sweet," I murmur. Her breathing grows ragged as she clings to me. My hard cock rubs against the inside of her legs as her dress bunches around her waist.

"That feels so good." Her whimpered moans drive me insane.

I capture her lips once more before pulling back. "You have any idea how long I've wanted to do that, Tatum?"

"Tell me," she whispers.

I brush loose strands of hair behind her ear. "So goddamn long."

"Are you sure you want to get involved with someone like me? Things could get messier," she states.

Gripping her chin, I stare into her beautiful ocean eyes. "You came along unexpectedly, and though the timing might have complicated things, it's nothing I can't handle, if you're willing."

She licks her lips and swallows hard. "I want to try."

"That's all I need to hear. We'll worry about the other stuff as it comes. We can get through it together," I reassure her.

"How are you so confident?"

"Thought you liked that about me?" I tease.

She rolls her eyes, grinning. "There's a lot of things I like about you."

I slowly slide my hands up her bare thighs. "Do tell."

Wrapping her arms around me and pulling me closer, she softly touches my lips. "You're so kind and caring. You make me laugh. You're protective yet not domineering. You're nice eye candy, too."

I chuckle, gripping behind her head and closing the little space left between us. My tongue swipes hers, and she moans. "Okay, now it's my turn."

She raises her brows as I brush a finger over her cheek. "All the things I like about you," I clarify. "Besides how drop-dead gorgeous you are, you light up the room every time you walk in one. You're resilient and strong. You're tough as nails, something I've noticed since the day we met. It's what drew me to you in the first place." I lean in and kiss her. "And staring at your fine ass all day was a bonus."

She snorts. "So you *are* an ass guy. My sister was right."

"Speaking of your sister, I should tell you something." I scratch along my jawline. "I *kinda* overheard your conversation last night."

Her eyes widen in horror. "Oh."

"I wasn't going to say anything, but since you mauled me before I could finish my cup of coffee, I figured I'd be up front."

She playfully smacks my chest. "I did *not* maul you."

I gently grab her wrist. "I'm gonna need to send Oakley a gift for snapping some sense into you."

"God, not you too." She playfully groans.

"It's okay to be scared, baby. You don't have to hold back your fears or concerns with me. All I ask is that you communicate."

"I'll try," she promises. "For the first time in a while, this feels right."

A sigh of contentment releases from my lips, and I press my forehead to hers. "I couldn't agree more."

Once Tatum and I finish talking and I drink my coffee, we hang out on the beach for a few hours. I slather her body with sunscreen and take every opportunity to kiss and touch her.

"I think I'm gonna take a shower," she tells me when we walk into the house.

"Me too, then I'll see what I can make for dinner. Any requests?"

"Something not burnt or covered in garlic powder," she sasses.

"Very funny." I give her ass a little smack. "I was thinking we should try out the hot tub tonight and watch the moonrise."

"I love that idea. Sounds very romantic," she says, wrapping her arms around my waist.

"I'm a romantic kind of guy."

"So I'm learning." She smirks, then leans in to kiss me. "I'll be down in twenty. Well, make it thirty."

I notice the hint of blush covering her cheeks. "Take your time."

Once she's upstairs, I quickly use the downstairs shower, then start dinner. We're getting low on groceries and will need to run to the store soon, but I manage to put together a chicken pasta dish. Per her request, no garlic.

"Wow, it smells delicious," she says, walking toward me.

I lower my eyes down her body, taking in the breathtaking sight in front of me. "You look amazing. I'm loving those sundresses on you." I pull her into my arms and kiss the tip of her nose. "Gonna be about fifteen to twenty minutes until dinner's ready. Just put it in the oven."

"Okay. Hmm...what could we do to pass the time?" She lingers adorably.

I bury my face in her neck and pepper kisses along her soft skin. Inhaling her fresh scent, I groan at what she's implying.

"Oh, I have *plenty* of ideas." I trace my tongue over her shoulder, sliding the strap down and exposing more of her chest. She's not wearing a bra, which gives me full access. Her nipples are hard. "Like starting with getting this out of the way."

"Wait..." She sucks in her lips, and I see the hesitation written on her face. "I have stretch marks."

"Tatum, I've seen you in a bikini already. You have nothing to worry about. I love them."

"How? I don't even *like* them," she argues.

"Because they're a part of you and your story. What you consider imperfections are what I can't stop fantasizing about. Every inch of you, I crave and want to devour."

Tears surface at the corners of her eyes, and I brush my thumb over them, then kiss both of her cheeks. "Up on the counter," I tell her, then lift her until she's comfortably seated.

"Are there cameras pointing this way?" she blurts out, suddenly aware that they could be watching us.

"No, they only aim toward the entryway of the house. The rest are outside," I reassure. "I thought you liked the idea of being watched?" I tease, sliding my hands down her body as I sink to the floor.

"I do...but maybe not by your brother and sister-in-law."

I chuckle in amusement. "Don't worry. The only one who's getting a private show is me." I flash her a wink, pushing her dress up and noticing she's completely bare. "No panties? Were you planning to seduce me?"

She playfully shrugs. "Truthfully, I'm out of underwear. I need to do laundry."

I chuckle at her honesty. "Lucky me."

As I kiss the inside of her thigh, I spread her legs apart and worship every inch I can get my lips on. She whimpers, and each moan she releases drives me crazy.

"I'm not sure I'll like that..." She glances down. "It's been a long, long time since I've had a man...*down there*."

Sadly, that doesn't surprise me.

"Don't be self-conscious. If I was any more obsessed with how much I want to taste you, you'd call me a freak."

"I just worry you won't like it."

"Are you nuts?"

She shrugs.

"I'm on my knees for you, baby. Let me worship you the way you deserve."

Tatum nods, giving me the permission I need. She grips her fingers on the edge of the counter and steadies herself.

"Keep your eyes on me."

Slowly, I kiss my way farther up, feeling her squirm with every lick and suck. I take my time as I make my way to her pussy.

"Fuck, baby. I can smell your arousal already." I swirl my finger through her wetness and groan.

Her breathing hitches as her head falls back.

"Eyes down here, Tatum," I demand.

She does what I say. "I want you to watch just how much I enjoy tasting you."

I inhale her scent before sliding my tongue between her folds. She hisses between her teeth and squirms against my face as I switch between licking and sucking her clit.

"How's that feel?" I ask.

"Intense and so, so good."

"Good. Hold on tight." I wink, then position one of her legs over my shoulder and sink back into her sweet cunt.

I flick my tongue over and over, creating buildup with every stroke and moan. Tatum's losing her ever-loving mind, and I can't get enough of her panting for more.

"You want my fingers, baby?" I ask for permission.

"Yes, *please*," she begs, breathing hard.

As I slowly slide a finger inside, I keep my eyes on hers. Her mouth opens, then I add another.

"Holy shit," she hisses. "That's amazing."

I smirk as I return to her clit and thrust two fingers in deep.

Her body convulses, and I know she's almost there. I keep my pace, feeling her pussy tighten around my knuckles.

"God, yes...*fuck*," she cries out, arching her hips as I continue flicking her clit. "Right there."

And like a bomb, she explodes.

"So goddamn beautiful when you come, baby," I tell her once I'm on my feet. "Wanna taste how sweet you are?"

All she can do is nod, and I smirk, bringing my mouth down on hers.

"I've never experienced anything like that," she says in awe. "I can't believe how good it was."

"Not bad for being a younger man, right?" I smirk, wiping my chin.

"For someone so sweet and caring, you sure are arrogant," she mocks, adjusting her dress over her hips.

"Only about things I'm confident about."

"Okay, well, I can't promise I'll be that good, but I want to return the favor." She notices the hard imprint of my cock through my jeans.

Before I can respond, the oven timer goes off.

Of fucking course.

I kiss her temple when she groans. "It's okay. I want to feed you first because you're gonna need the energy for what I have planned for us tonight."

CHAPTER SIXTEEN

TATUM

MY LIMBS FEEL like Jell-O after Easton gave me the orgasm of the century. I truly never knew it could be this way. Although I wanted to pleasure him, I was glad for the break so my heart could catch up to my head. I'm not sexually experienced beyond missionary and want nothing more than to make him feel good. Justin was the only man I had been with, but he stopped putting my needs first, even before our marriage fell apart.

But that doesn't mean I don't want to try. They say it's just like riding a bicycle, right?

I wish I was bold enough to text Oakley for tips, but I'm not ready to open that box. She doesn't need all the dirty details, though she'd ask for them.

"Ready to get in the hot tub?" Easton asks after we eat and clean the kitchen.

"Umm...hold on. Can you sit on the couch for me?" I ask nervously.

He pops a brow. "Sure."

I adore how he's so willing to just go with whatever I ask. He has the patience of a saint.

Once he's settled, I stand between his legs and kneel. He wraps his hands behind his head, giving me full access to him.

"I want you to tell me what you want me to do," I tell him.

"Undo my button and zipper," he commands with fire in his eyes, and I do. I keep my gaze locked on his, ready and willing. "Lower my jeans and pull out my cock."

I slowly unzip as I anticipate seeing him. Easton doesn't rush me. He stays silent and patient as I nervously fumble my way through it.

With both hands, I pull down his pants as he lifts his hips to help. His thick cock springs free, and my mouth waters at the sight of it.

Good Lord.

"Now what?" I ask hoarsely.

"Spit on it and stroke my shaft," he orders.

Bringing the tip to my lips, I spit over the crown. When it's nice and slippery, I grip him, then slowly stroke up and down. He releases a groan, and I move faster, the friction of my hand and his velvety skin making him harder.

The thick vein under his shaft bulges, and it's obvious he likes the way it feels.

"Wrap those pretty lips around my cock, Tatum. Suck hard, slow, fast, deep—however you want. I promise it'll feel amazing no matter what you do."

He knows I need reassurance, and I appreciate that he doesn't make me question myself.

Sitting up higher on my knees, I bring his tip to my mouth and open. He smells so manly, and I can't get enough. I inhale, then push him inside me.

Easton releases a moan that encourages me to keep going. His fingers tangle in my hair as he slowly guides me up and down his length.

"Play with my balls with your other hand," he grits out.

I nudge his legs wider with my elbow and reach between his thighs.

"Careful," he adds. "They're sensitive."

As softly as I can, I cup and massage them as I stroke and suck on his cock. Saliva is all over my chin and fingers as I go deeper.

"Fuck, Tatum...that's perfect. You're working me so goddamn good."

His compliments fill my stomach with butterflies, and I want nothing more than to help him lose control.

Every time I squeeze my lips around him, he buckles underneath me. I stroke him harder as I hollow my cheeks, noticing how it drives him crazy.

"Shit, baby. I'm gonna come. Move back."

This time, though, I *don't* listen.

I tighten my grip and increase my pace. If he can eat me out and lick my arousal, I can swallow his.

"Tatum..." He runs his fingers through my hair and gently tugs, but I stay planted. "*Fuck.*"

With a guttural groan, his thighs shake against me as he releases down my throat. I swallow him down, loving how he tastes. Licking my lips, I meet his satisfied gaze. Easton cups my face, and our mouths collide. He groans, pulling me on his lap, then cups my ass.

"Best fucking blow job I've ever had," he murmurs.

I snort. "Doubtful."

"Swear to God, Tatum. You kneeling between my legs with my cock in your mouth is a vision I'll never forget."

I feel the same about the way he ate me out in the kitchen.

My bare pussy grinds against his erection. I shift slightly to see if he notices.

"*Tatum*..." he warns as he grips my hips to stop me.

"Oh sorry, you probably need an hour to, uh..." I nod toward his groin.

He snaps his eyes to me, disbelief in them. Then he bursts out laughing. "Oh, woman. I'm about to blow your damn mind and show you *exactly* why being with a younger man is gonna be the best experience of your life."

My heart skips a beat at his arrogant tone.

"But I did promise you a date night in the hot tub so we could watch the moonrise."

Seriously? He wants to stop? We can go in the hot tub any other night.

"You look disappointed." He brushes my hair back, then buries his face in my neck. "Is that because you liked my tongue in your pussy?"

A shiver rolls through me. "Yes," I whisper.

"What else do you want in that tight little cunt of yours?"

The way those sexy words fall from his mouth like he's asking about the weather boggles my mind. His confidence intimidates me, but I can't let my insecurities get in the way of what I really want.

Him. *All of him.*

"You," I say when he cups my breast.

"No, I want to hear you say it. Tell me *exactly* what you want me to do to you." He pinches a nipple, causing my head to spin.

I swallow hard, finding every ounce of courage I have left. Not only has no man ever asked me that question but I've also never experienced foreplay dirty talk. Have to admit I love it.

Easton's intense gaze almost has me chickening out, but then I remembered a couple of romance books I read recently. All the heroines took charge of their sex lives and weren't afraid to admit what they wanted from their partners. It was empowering to see these women find love and the man of their dreams. If they could, then so can I.

"I want you to want me as much as I want you."

"Already done, my love. I've been infatuated with you since the moment we met. That turned to an addiction to see you every chance I could, and now I'm obsessed. I *need* you in my life. Have no doubt that my world revolves around you completely."

"Those are some really strong words," I admit, on the edge of an emotional breakdown.

"I'm sorry if I admitted that too soon, but I'll always be up front with you, Tatum."

He swipes my cheeks, and I feel foolish for crying. There's no reason I need to be this emotional. But again, no one's ever told me anything like this before. I've never been someone's *world*.

"Then I should be honest with you," I say, clearing my throat. "I've had a crush on you since the start but hid it for obvious reasons. I've been slowly falling for you a little more each day since we've been in this house together, and I can no longer ignore it."

"That's the most amazing thing I've ever heard." He smiles, pulling my lips to his.

"I really want this," I mutter, giving us both reassurance.

"Thank fuck, because I want your body, mind, and anything else you'll give me."

I chuckle, grinding down on his lap and feeling him grow hard again.

"But not here. I want you in my bed," he says. "I want to show you exactly what I see when I look at you."

Huh? I have no idea what that means, but I climb off his lap so we can readjust our clothes, then he leads me upstairs.

"You see that full-length mirror in the corner?" He points at the white-framed one angled between the walls.

I nod, unsure of where he's going with this.

He takes my hand and moves me in front of it. As Easton stands behind me, he squeezes my arms and smiles at our reflection.

"I want you to see what I find so beautiful about you," he murmurs in my ear as he slides my dress over my head. I wasn't wearing any undergarments, so I'm naked.

"Don't hide from me, Tatum," he says when I instinctively cross my arms to cover myself. "These tits fit perfectly in my palm. I'd be lying if I said I haven't been fantasizing about them bouncing in my face while you ride me. I can't fucking wait to experience that with you." I moan when he cups my breast and pinches a nipple. "I might be an ass man, but these are a close second."

I chuckle as my cheeks heat. Looking at myself is a form of self-torture, right next to standing on a scale.

"I also love this little dip down your stomach. I want to trace my tongue between your breasts and down to your pussy. The perfect trail."

My stomach is on the slimmer side, but my hips are wide. I gained a little weight with my last pregnancy, but then I gained even more when the depression of losing the baby hit. Though I've lost a little, there's still some around my midsection.

"And don't even get me started on this fine ass of yours." He slaps one cheek, then rubs the burn. "It's a cruel temptation I've tried not to stare at for the past two months."

I smirk at the way he growls.

"Your strong thighs were made to straddle my face."

I fight back the urge to laugh. He means my thick thunder

thighs. The very ones Justin despised so much because they were chunky and covered in cellulite.

"But you're so much more than all of that, Tatum. Your *heart*..." He presses his palm to the middle of my chest. "That's the most beautiful part of you."

Meeting his gaze in the mirror, I find his expression filled with pure sincerity.

"Now do you see what I see?" He grips my chin and turns my head to face him. "Do you see why I desire you?"

"No one's ever made me feel as wanted as you, and it's overwhelming. I've been ashamed of my body for so long. It's going to take me a while to love it as much as you do."

The corner of his lips tilts up. "Fair enough. That just means I get to remind you until you do. Whatever it takes to heal every emotional and physical scar you have, I'll do it till the day I die."

I reach up and crash my mouth to his. I'm no longer falling for this man. I've straight up tripped and fell off the ledge, heart first into his arms.

Without another word, I reach for his zipper and pull down his jeans. He releases me to remove his clothes. As soon as he's naked, I take in every glorious inch.

Sweet Jesus. Not only is he younger but he's also rock hard all over.

"From this moment on, I'm yours, and you're mine. I don't want you second-guessing a thing when it comes to how I feel about you."

"You're very possessive," I say with an amused grin.

"*Protective*," he counters. "The only time I'll control you is when you ask me to. Otherwise, you're in charge, baby."

I have no idea how to be *in charge*, but I have a feeling I'm going to like exploring it.

CHAPTER SEVENTEEN

EASTON

I WAIT for Tatum to make a move, and when she stares blankly up at me, I know she's out of her comfort zone when it comes to asking for what she wants.

"Tell me what you want me to do, and I'll do it," I tell her.

"I want you to make me lose control."

Instead of asking her to elaborate, I press our mouths together and guide her to the bed. She lies down, and I tower over her, placing a knee between her legs.

"Show me how you touch yourself."

Her doe eyes meet mine.

"Or do you need your vibrator?" I grin.

"I mean, if you don't think you can do the job, sure."

"That's hilarious. You know damn well I can. And I *will*. Over and over until you beg me to stop. Until you lose your voice from screaming all night, and your body is limp from pleasure."

She gulps, and it causes me to laugh.

"So I'll say it again...show me how you make yourself come."

"There's that bossy tone I've grown used to," she taunts, moving a hand down to her pussy.

Slowly, she rubs circles over her clit, and I watch as the buildup makes her squirm. I slide a finger down her slit until it's covered in her juices, then thrust it inside her. She gasps and spreads her legs wider.

"Don't stop," I tell her when she slows her pace. "Focus on me, baby."

Her blue eyes find mine, and together, we bring her over the edge. She exhales as I pull out. Then I grab the back of her thighs and pull her legs around me so I can align myself to her entrance.

"Yours," I remind her.

"Mine," she confirms, and then I grip my shaft and slowly push inside.

We groan at the same time as the pleasure consumes us. I wait for her to get used to my size, and once I'm all the way in, I blow out a satisfied breath.

"Goddamn, your cunt is tight," I murmur against her lips. "Are you okay?"

She nods as she arches her hips up to meet mine. "It's so good."

"Fucking right it is." Lifting her leg higher allows me to slide in deeper. Tatum's eyes roll to the back of her head as she fists the covers.

I explore every inch of her that I can touch. Her supple breasts and hard nipples, her swollen clit, and her neck that I want to mark with my mouth. We move in rhythm as I adjust our position and lift her hips above my knees.

"I'm so close," she tells me.

"Mmm...you're squeezing me so hard, and it feels amazing. Come on my cock, Tatum. Don't hold back."

I increase my pressure on her red bud, and moments later,

her legs tighten around my waist as her body convulses. Her wetness glides down my length as she screams out her release.

"You have no idea how goddamn sexy that was. Christ, you're beautiful." I lower my mouth to hers as she catches her breath. "Sorry to tell you, but I'm not anywhere near done with you."

"I'm so glad I started doing yoga a few months ago."

"You and me both." I chuckle. "Another first of yours I get to claim."

She blushes. "Arrogant much?"

"No. Now get on top of me."

She moves over so I can lie down and watch in excitement as she straddles me. "One of your fantasies was me riding you?" she asks.

I reach up and cup her breasts. "Lived rent free in my head nearly every day."

"Guess we should make it a reality then." She flashes me a devilish smile, then grabs my shaft and coats it in her wetness. I watch as she lines it up between her legs and slides down my length. I can already see her confidence growing.

I hiss out a curse as she begins rocking and giving me the best view I've ever seen. Leaning up, I capture her breast and kiss her chest. Rounding a hand to her backside, I give her ass a little slap.

"Take what you need from me. My cock is yours. Fuck *me*, baby."

She widens her hips and grinds harder against me.

"Good girl." I smile against her neck.

"It's so intense," she admits as I squeeze her hips and increase the friction between us.

"Just like the feelings I have for you," I say, pressing my lips to her shoulder.

She pushes against my chest, making me fall back on the mattress. A giggle releases when she sees my shocked face.

"I wanna ride you in the reverse cowgirl position. I read about it in one of my books, and I've never done it before," she explains before turning around and shoving her luscious ass in my face. There's no way she would've been comfortable in this position even days ago, and knowing she is tells me she feels safe with me.

Okay, I lied. *This* is the best view of my life.

I dig my fingers in her ass cheeks and guide her over my cock until I'm seated deep inside. She leans forward and holds my legs for support, then begins moving up and down.

This new angle is tight enough to make me blow my load before I'm ready. I lift my hips to meet her thrusts, and we groan out in pleasure.

When I feel how close she is, I spank her, and she yelps. "Keep going, sweetheart. Ride that dick. You're almost there."

Tatum moans as the buildup takes over, and her thighs shake through the pleasure. She coats my cock again, and it takes all the willpower in the world not to spill inside her.

When she comes down from her high, she falls against my shins and catches her breath.

"Don't tell me you're worn out already?" I taunt, pulling her up next to me.

"Whatever you're on, it's enough."

I bark out a laugh. "I didn't take anything nor have I ever."

"Sweet Jesus. So it's *always* like this?"

Scratching my cheek, I smirk at how shocked she sounds. "My poor girl. So damn sex-deprived, your expectations were on the floor."

"I finally understand what all those female characters mean when they say they're going to die of sex overload."

"Not possible," I counter.

"No, I really think it is. My heart's about to beat out of my chest."

Chuckling, I press my mouth to hers. "Try to keep up. I'm not finished with you."

I stand and hold out my hand. Once she takes it, I lead her back to the mirror.

"Now look at yourself. All flushed and glistening."

"Like a glazed donut," she repeats my words from when she taught me yoga, and I chuckle.

"Tastes sweet like one too." I wink. "Put your palms on the wall and spread your legs."

"What? Why?"

"You trust me?" I brush my lips to her ear. "You don't have to do anything you don't want."

She swallows and nods. "Of course I do." I watch as she gets into position.

Standing behind her, I bring a hand between her thighs, and she's wet again. Tatum pants as I finger-fuck her, and when her head falls back on my shoulder, I stop.

"Watch," I demand.

Her eyes pop open, and they meet mine in the reflection.

"I want you to see what I see. Watch us in the mirror."

She does as I say and flicks her gaze forward. She focuses on my fingers moving in and out as she tries to catch her breath.

I slide out, then press down on her lower back until she's angled just right.

"Watch," I remind her, gripping my shaft and teasing her entrance.

Tatum spreads her thighs wider, giving me the access I need to thrust in. Her ass cheeks bounce as I slam against her over and over. Taking her from behind allows me to go to the hilt, and based on her rapid breathing, she likes it.

"Don't you look stunning with my cock stuffed inside you?" I watch her expression in the mirror and know she's trying to focus, but her eyes keep rolling back.

"Tatum."

Her gaze finds mine.

"You're beautiful," I mouth.

My balls tighten, and I know I'm close to exploding.

"I'm almost there, baby. Where do you want it?"

She grins. "On my chest."

Fuck, she's perfect.

"On your knees," I order.

Quickly, she spins around as I stroke my shaft. When Tatum focuses on me, I'm done. The orgasm rips through me, and soon, I'm releasing all over her beautiful tits. With a satisfied groan, I drop my arms to my sides.

"Holy *shit*."

"That was a lot." She chuckles, looking down.

"I know." Grabbing her hand, I pull her up to her feet. "Let's get in the shower." I press a kiss to her lips on the way to the bathroom.

"I have a feeling I'm gonna need some painkillers, or I might not be able to walk tomorrow," she says as I get the water going.

"The fact that you're able to walk right now means we haven't found our limit yet."

She blinks wide. "Excuse you? I didn't think I was *that* old until just now. There are *more* than three rounds?"

Smirking, I brush the sweaty strands of hair off her forehead and press a soft kiss there. "I can't wait to show you all the amazing ways I'm going to make you feel good."

"Maybe I should stretch next time."

I laugh, guiding her under the warm stream of water. "Well you know what they say, practice makes progress."

"I thought it was practice makes perfect?"

"There's no such thing as perfect, except for when it comes to you."

She rolls her eyes. "That was corny, even for you."

I playfully slap her ass, and she yelps. "That's what you get, naughty girl."

That night, we shared a bed for the first time. Now that I've had her, I'm not letting her go. She slept pressed up against my chest and snored so adorably. She was knocked out within ten minutes of lying down. I soon followed.

Tatum stirs next to me, but when she snores moments later, I know she's still passed out. Kissing the top of her head, I carefully crawl out from under the covers and go to the bathroom. It's nine in the morning, and the sun is glaring through the windows. It's gonna be another hot and humid day.

Once I'm dressed and head downstairs, I look through the fridge and pantry. Before I can decide on what I'm making for breakfast, my phone rings, and I see it's from Detective Hansen, who took over my case.

"Hello," I greet, and he lets me know there's been an update. I pace the dining room.

"We've confirmed the cause of the fire to your shop and home was arson. Noticeable flame patterns led us to gasoline trails. The person who did this knew how to trip your security system and get in without being heard."

I grind my teeth and rub a hand over my face. "Okay, so now what?"

"Well, we secured footage from a few different businesses in the area, including one that's behind the alley. It showed a man with a couple of gas cans around the time the fire broke out. We've identified him as Justin Nichols."

Holy shit, I knew it!

"Really? Wow. Has he been arrested?" I ask, trying to calm my nerves.

"There's a warrant out for his arrest, but he hasn't been located."

Fuck.

"Are they going to be looking for him in Nebraska as well?"

"Yes, and the police department has been briefed, considering his position there. Unfortunately, he hasn't shown up to work in a few weeks."

"His ex's lawyer said Justin was meeting with him this upcoming week. He should be there," I explain. After I realized I could trust the detective, I opened up about Tatum working at the shop and living in the apartment upstairs.

"Do you know what day and time?"

I brush my fingers through my hair as I try to recall. "No, I'd have to ask."

"I'll make a note to reach out to the attorney," he says.

"I really appreciate you calling to give me an update."

"You're welcome. I'll call you when we have him. Stay safe, okay?"

"Got it."

My mind spins when we hang up.

Tatum isn't going to like this. She'll go back to blaming herself and being scared that Justin is on the loose. Right now, he could be anywhere.

He could be watching us right now.

After I make us peanut butter toast, I bring it up to her and gently wake her.

"Good morning," I whisper, bringing my lips to her ear. "I made you something to eat."

"Hmm..." She groans. "It doesn't smell like steak and eggs."

I chuckle, brushing her wild hair off her face. "Not even close. But I have some news I need to share with you."

That makes her eyes pop open, and I quickly give her a smile. She sits up, and I hand her the plate. She eats while I explain the conversation with Detective Hansen.

"Well, he's gotta be in Nebraska," she states with certainty. "My attorney said they were meeting Tuesday. That's in two days."

"That's what I told him. He hasn't shown up for work in a few weeks, but they're looking for him."

She dazes out for a few moments. "So does that mean he could still be here?"

"I don't know, sweetheart. He might be on the run and across the country by now."

"One could only hope."

"Please don't worry."

"I'm trying not to, but I'd like for us to go grocery shopping without having to look over my shoulder."

"I won't let him touch you, Tatum."

Her face falls. "I know, but I get scared he could hurt you."

I scoff. "I'd take a bullet, knife, punch in the face—whatever—for you."

"Oh yeah, that's gonna help me not worry *at all*." She groans, and I chuckle.

"Don't let him ruin our day. We can't control what happens, so let's not dwell on it. Our apartments will eventually be rebuilt, and we can get back to our lives."

She leans in, and I brush my lips against hers.

"I was thinking I'd FaceTime Oakley. She's dying to meet you. It might be time."

I arch a brow. "Yeah? Sweet. I'd love to."

"Fair warning, she's a handful."

"So are you, sweetheart." I flash her a wink.

CHAPTER EIGHTEEN

TATUM

DAY 24

THIS PAST WEEK with Easton has been amazing, especially since we've barely left the bedroom. However, I've been stressed about Justin's disappearance. To keep my mind off things, Easton has given me two surfing lessons. I'm excited by how far I'm progressing. He's extremely patient with me and hands out tons of compliments. I'm getting stronger and more confident on the board too, which makes me happy.

When I think about everything that's happened, I'm so damn thankful I listened to Oakley's advice and gave him a chance. I didn't realize how good it could feel to be with someone who cares so much about me. Just another reminder of how terrible my marriage was.

"Are you almost ready?" Easton asks from the doorway.

"How do I look?" I'm standing in my bra and panties with a full face of makeup. My hair is pulled up into a ponytail.

"If you left the house looking like that…" He tucks his bottom lip into his mouth. "Actually, what am I saying? We'd never leave."

Easton takes two steps forward and brushes his soft lips to mine. I'll never get sick of him or how he pours all of his emotions into me any time we're close.

When we finally pull away, I'm breathless. "You're kinda convincing me to stay home."

"Nah, you're going to love the boardwalk festival. It's a lot of fun. Remember what we promised each other?"

With a grin, I repeat our agreement after I learned Justin didn't show up to meet with my lawyer. "Yes. That we won't let my shitty ex ruin our time together, and we're going to enjoy the rest of the summer."

Easton nods. "That's right. Pretty sure if he were still in Florida, he would've already been caught or made his move."

I suck in a deep breath. "You're right. Plus, it will be nice to get out."

"Yes, so get dressed." Easton grabs a handful of my ass and leans in to kiss my neck.

"Stop teasing me!" I playfully swat his chest. "Or we're staying in."

He pulls back with a grin, then walks out. Quickly, I slip on a pair of shorts and a racerback tank top, then meet him downstairs.

He's wearing board shorts and a light green T-shirt that really brings out the color of his eyes.

"I'm going to have to fight off all the ladies today, aren't I?"

He tilts his head at me. "The only woman I want is standing right in front of me."

Easton wraps his arms around me, then places a sweet kiss on my forehead. "If anything, I'm going to be fighting dudes off you. You're sexy as hell, baby."

I scoff but can't help smiling at his sweet words. Easton pulls away and grabs a few bottles of water and then we go to his car. We make small talk, and by the time we get to town, I realize how big of a deal this summer celebration is. A ton of booths are set up along the sidewalk, plus many food trucks and activities. Somehow, he finds a parking spot that's not too far away from all of the commotion.

He turns and glances in the back seat. "Ready to make that fantasy come true?"

My eyes widen when I realize what he's referring to. My sex bucket list.

"Right now?"

"Only if you want to." He smirks, and I quickly nod.

We get out of the front seats and make our way to the back. As soon as he locks the doors, Easton's hands and lips are on mine. Thankfully, the windows are tinted, but if anyone focuses on the car, they'll know exactly what's going on. Especially if they watch from the front windshield. The thought sparks arousal between my thighs.

When I unzip Easton's shorts, his cock springs to life. I place my mouth around the tip, sucking and coating his shaft. He wraps my ponytail around his fist, moaning and giving me positive reinforcements as he guides himself to the back of my throat.

"Fuck, you're so good at that," he whisper-hisses. "Ride me, baby. I need to be inside you."

In the confines of the back seat, I wiggle out of my shorts and panties. The reality of what we're doing drives me wild, and I can feel how soaking wet I am. Slowly, I glide down his thick cock and let him fill me full. As I rock my hips, he peels up my shirt and bra and flicks my hard nipples.

I run my fingers through his hair as I bounce hard and fast on his dick. Easton rubs his thumb over my clit, and my eyes bolt open when I hear voices nearby.

"Do you think they can see us?" I ask between ragged breaths. I'm starting to sweat as our bodies slap together.

"Probably. At the very least, they can see the car rocking. I kinda hope they can, though. If we are being *watched*…I hope he sees how fucking sexy you are riding me. Hope he can see me squeeze your breast and flick your clit. Hope he sees how worked up I make you. And I hope he sees how goddamn amazing you look taking my cock."

I know exactly who he's referring to. If Justin is stalking me, he's getting a full NC-17 show. He'll see a man take care of me the way he never could. If it were up to Easton, he'd find a way to take him out for good, but I only want him out of my life so I can move on without fear. Though I do appreciate the way Easton is ready and willing to harm anyone who acts as a threat.

I nod in agreement, and as our lips crash together, the orgasm builds. He continues rubbing circles with one hand, then reaches behind and puts one in my tight hole. My head falls back on my shoulders, and I don't know how much longer I'll be able to last before I lose control. More people pass by, and within seconds, my entire body shakes and seizes.

"Oh my God, Easton," I scream out my release, not caring who can hear me. I come so hard he has to steady me.

"Fuck," he whisper-hisses as my pussy nearly squeezes off his dick. Just by his slowed movements, I can tell that he's close. Easton grabs my ass cheeks, creating more friction, and soon, he's losing himself inside me. We wrap our arms around each other as we steady our breathing. Eventually, I open my eyes and meet his intense ones.

"That orgasm nearly blinded me," I admit.

He steals a kiss. "You enjoyed that fantasy."

I wiggle against him. "I did. The risk of being seen or caught. The thought of him watching us and you claiming me. Shit, I'm getting worked up all over again just thinking about it."

He chuckles. "I adore this version of you, baby. And don't worry, I enjoyed it too. Oh, I brought a towel," he tells me, pointing at it on the floorboard.

"Oh thank goodness."

Once we're cleaned and dressed, Easton reaches forward and turns on the car, then blasts the A/C. I try to cool down as we stretch out in the back seat.

"Guess I can mark that one off the list," I beam.

"Next up is Germany."

I chuckle.

"Then we can fuck in the plane bathroom on our way home."

He hums. "You're getting me hard again, babe."

I squeeze my legs together. "I'm already aching for more of you."

He chuckles. "I can *never* get enough." He leans in, sliding his tongue between my lips. We make out some more, and I'm tempted to ride him again, but I know we should get going before someone really does see us. The quicker we enjoy this festival, the sooner we can go home and fool around.

Easton intertwines his fingers with mine as we head down the sidewalk with flustered faces and swollen lips. I can feel every place he's been this past week, and there's not a chance in hell I ever want to give that up. He knows my body better than anyone.

"You good?" he asks when we get closer to the festivities. It's been a while since I've been in a crowded place.

"Yeah, I'm fine. Knowing there's a warrant out for Justin's arrest makes me feel safer. He won't be out in the open and risk getting caught, even if he's here. He's not that stupid."

"If he is, there'd be hundreds of witnesses," Easton admits.

I nod.

Leaning in, he whispers, "I have to admit that having you

come on my dick with the possibility of your ex-husband watching turned me on even more." His mouth traces the shell of my ear, and goose bumps trail over my body. My pussy throbs just thinking about it.

I lean in and speak softly. "If he did see, I'm sure his ego's bruised that you made me come."

Before he can pull away, I place my hand on his cheek and crash my mouth against his. He smiles against my lips. "You're mine, baby. I will worship your sweet little cunt until the day I die," he states for only me to hear.

My eyes flutter open. "I love the sound of that."

Easton takes my hand again, and we make our way down the sidewalk, stopping to look at all the craft tables.

"Oh my goodness!" I gasp when I see a necklace made of sea glass.

"Yeah, this is what I was talking about! Do you see one you like?"

"They're all beautiful."

He reaches forward and grabs one with turquoise-colored glass, then steps behind me and puts it around my neck. "Beautiful."

"That one looks great on you," the woman says, and I can see she's wearing one almost identical to mine.

"We'll take it." Easton pulls out his wallet and hands her the money.

"I love it. Thank you so much," I tell him.

"You're very welcome. It's a crime to leave a summer festival without picking up something cool and handmade."

"I'm still not used to this," I admit as he takes my hand in his again and brings them up to his lips.

"You will soon." He winks.

We stop at a few painter's booths, and I admire the beautifully illustrated beach scenes on canvas.

"Do you think Oakley could recreate something like this?" Easton asks when we move to the next table.

"My sister could probably whip it up in her sleep. She's an incredible painter and has more talent in her pinky finger than I have in my whole body."

He snorts. "That's how siblings always feel."

"But this time, it's actually true."

"You'll have to show me her work sometime because I know exactly how much *talent* you have in that sexy body." He waggles his brows.

I snort. "You'll be impressed. I still don't know how she does it so flawlessly."

We look at wind chimes, furniture made from recycled beach wood, firepits, and tons of handmade clothing booths. Everything reminds me of the perfect summer day.

Easton and I talk about random things as we walk around. I love how he wraps his arm around me when we stop to look at something. It still gives me butterflies—another thing I'm not used to.

A shop is selling bikinis, and Easton stops. "What about this one?" he asks, holding up a bathing suit made from shoestrings.

"I don't think it would cover me." I shake my head.

"That's the point." The woman behind the table laughs.

"He's right," she offers. "And right now, they're buy one, get one free."

"Oh you're tempting me now," Easton says, waving it in front of me.

"You should pick out one and let your wife pick out the other," she suggests.

My cheeks heat at hearing her call me that.

She must notice because she adds, "Oh I'm sorry. I shouldn't have assumed."

"It's okay. She will be one day." He flashes me a knowing wink.

The words *one day* linger in the air, and my heart flutters at the thought of being married to him. Everything's happening so fast, but I wouldn't hesitate to spend the rest of my life with him.

Looking through the racks, I find one that's completely mesh. It's sexy. "I like this one."

Easton lifts a brow and smirks, holding up his choice too. "Can't wait for you to model these for me," he says, leaning in and biting the flesh on my neck.

The woman smiles as he pays, then hands me the black sack.

"You're spoiling me too much," I say to Easton as we continue down the boardwalk. "You better stop before I get used to it."

"Never. I like to spoil you, Tatum. In and out of the bedroom."

A laugh escapes me.

"Want a snow cone?"

"Ooh, yes, please! I can't remember the last time I had one."

"Which flavor?"

I smile as I read over the options. "Hm…surprise me."

"You should stand over there in the shade. This line is kinda long," Easton suggests, and I nod. The sun is beaming down, and I'm starting to sweat. We forgot sunscreen too.

I watch him as he waits patiently to order. Though I told Oakley what we were doing when we chatted yesterday, I want to let her know how it's been so far. It's the first time we've been a couple out in public, and it's felt so damn right and natural.

Pulling out my phone, I turn toward the shade to avoid the

glare on the screen. Before I can even click on her name, I feel Easton's mouth on the shell of my ear, and I lean into him.

"Missed me, you fucking whore?"

My spine straightens as I recognize Justin's voice. Before I can scream or turn around, something hard is shoved into my back, and I know it's his gun.

"One motherfucking peep, and I'll kill your little boy toy. Then I'll put a bullet between your eyes. How old is he anyway? Is he even legal to drive?"

"Fuck you," I whisper-hiss. Rage consumes me as I curse myself for letting my guard down.

"You thought you really did something when you fucked him in the back of a car for everyone to see, huh?" He leans in close, smelling my hair. "What a goddamn whore my wife is."

I cringe at his words. "Not anymore," I spit out, fumbling with my cell phone to dial 911.

"Shut the fuck up and start walking," he growls, shoving the barrel harder into my skin and guiding me farther away from Easton.

When he gets into a rage like this, there's no talking him out of it. I have to do exactly what he says so he'll at least leave Easton alone.

"You think you're so fuckin' smart, don't you? You really thought I wouldn't find you? I've been watching you, Tatum. I always knew you were dense, but I didn't realize how much of a stupid bitch you are too." He stays close so no one suspects anything. People passing by are hardly paying us a glance.

My mind is shutting down as my fight response fails on me once again. All the horrible things he's done to me over the years come flooding back, and I'm that weak person all over again. I manage to press the call button without him noticing. I won't be able to tell them my location, but maybe they can track me.

"Tatum!" I hear Easton call from behind a few times, his voice sounding closer each time he yells my name. *Shit.*

Justin speeds us up. "Your stupid dildo is gonna get hurt trying to rescue you."

I try to break free and yank out of his grip, but his nails dig into my arm so damn tight, I know I'll bruise.

Justin spins us around just as Easton comes into view.

"No!" I scream at him. "Stop!"

Justin bellows out an evil laugh, and it brings chills up my spine as he chambers a round. The sound of clicking makes me sick because I know what he's capable of.

"He has a gun!" I scream as Easton sprints toward us.

Justin backhands me. "Shut the fuck up."

My cheek stings as he grabs my arm again and forces me to keep walking away. No one's stopped to help or get involved.

"Don't do this, Justin," I try to barter with him.

It only pisses him off more. He grabs a fistful of my ponytail and yanks hard. "Say another word and—"

Before Justin can continue, Easton collides with us from behind, and the three of us fall to the ground.

"Tatum, run," Easton pleads before I even have the chance to get up. By the time I can, Easton throws a punch in Justin's face. It hardly fazes him, and seconds later, Justin whacks Easton across the face with his gun.

"Stop it!" I scream at Justin. He leans over him, ready to deliver another blow when Easton kicks out his foot and trips him. They're rolling around, swinging and kicking.

Fumbling to find my phone, I find it on the ground behind me and dial 911 again.

People finally realize something's wrong and move toward us, the altercation becoming the main attraction.

"911, what's your location?"

"Uhh…the summer festival," I stutter out frantically. "Off Winnebago Ave."

Before I can continue, Justin gets to his feet and spits out blood. Then he points his gun at Easton.

I drop my phone, ready to beg him not to hurt him. "Justin, no, please."

"I'll fucking kill you both." He turns the gun on me.

Three seconds later, a piercing gunshot rings out, and I scream out in horror.

CHAPTER NINETEEN

EASTON

JUSTIN COLLAPSES to the ground before I can comprehend what just happened. Tatum stands ten feet away in shock. Then I notice blood next to Justin.

"Easton!" Tatum rushes over, kneeling beside me. "Are you okay?"

"I'm fine, baby."

"You're bleeding," she tells me, and I touch my cheek. Then I notice red marks on her face where the bastard hit her.

People circle around us, and I get to my feet, pulling Tatum close.

We both look at Justin's lifeless body in shock.

"What in the hell just happened?"

She shakes her head and lets out a wail of a cry as she wraps her arms around my neck. "I was so worried he was going to kill you."

"I know. I'm fine. I'm here, baby," I tell her, wrapping her in a tight hug. As people crowd us, I see a man walk up carrying a sniper rifle. I hurry and push Tatum behind me, not willing to let anyone else try to take her from me. If I die, so be it.

The guy is enormous, a burly man with a thick, dark beard.

He looks like he came out of a lumberjack magazine. His black eyes meet mine as I wait for him to point the gun at me. Instead, he holds out his hand, which confuses the hell out of me.

"Are you two okay?" he asks in a raspy, deep voice as he drops his hand since I didn't take it.

"Yeah," I drawl slowly. "Who are you?"

"My friends call me Bear. I'm a friend of Tristan's."

Instantly, the tension fizzles. "My *brother*?"

"Yeah. He hired me to watch you guys because apparently, you'd use *kung fu* or some bullshit if someone attacked you. His words, not mine."

My mouth falls open. "That son of a bitch." I can't believe he never told me he hired someone. "How long have you been following us?"

"Just a couple of weeks. You guys hardly left the house, so it made my job pretty easy."

I snort. I have so many questions, but I'll drill Tristan later.

"Good thing I was here. Not sure how that would've ended otherwise," he tells me.

"Yeah, you're telling me. I turn my back for five seconds…" I grit between my teeth, angry with myself for not keeping Tatum glued to my side.

Bear turns and looks at Justin. "He's dead."

"Yeah," I say, shielding Tatum from seeing the gruesome image. Sirens can be heard in the distance, so I know they'll be here within minutes.

Tatum angles her head slightly to look at Bear. "You're really good at your job. I had no idea."

"That's the point. Tristan didn't want you to know. Stay out of sight until I'm needed. He was concerned about you two."

"He saved our lives," Tatum whispers, and I nod.

"I know, we'll call him later," I tell her, rubbing my hand slowly down her back.

Once the fire trucks and police cars arrive, more people rush over. They're gasping and holding out their cell phones to record. Finally, the emergency responders arrive and push their way through the crowd.

"Alright, back up, everyone. We need to secure the scene," an officer shouts, waving people back.

A few of them rush over to Justin and check his pulse. One of them looks up at another officer and shakes their head. It's pure chaos of officers and EMTs.

"Can someone please tell me what happened here? Who are the witnesses?" another officer asks.

Bear steps up, giving his account for what he saw and who he is. He did everything by the book and even has a body cam to prove what happened.

"When Justin pulled his gun and aimed it at the victim, I took my shot," he tells the officer. "He'd been threatening Ms. Benson with it on her back while he walked her out of the area, but I followed and waited before assessing the situation. Once it became life-threatening, I couldn't wait any longer."

The way he describes the scene has my mind reeling because he's absolutely right. This could've ended a lot differently. Just thinking about it makes me shudder.

They ask Bear to come down to the station to prove his credentials and write a formal witness statement.

Moments later, the officers ask for Tatum's and my account of the events. She tells them everything she knows, from their marriage to my shop burning down, the restraining order, and finally, the warrant they have out for his arrest. The officer looks at her like she's lying. After telling them everything, I realize how much shit Tatum's gone through and how horrible it must've been dealing with a manipulative spouse for so long. My heart aches for her all over again.

Once we exchange information with the detective, we're allowed to leave.

When we turn around, there's a barrier around Justin's body. I watch as Tatum stares at him. "I didn't want it to end this way," she murmurs.

I wrap an arm around her waist and pull her close. "I know, sweetheart." She's way too kind to even wish death upon a man who tried to kill her.

"Thank you again," I tell Bear before I take Tatum's hand. "I don't know how to repay you for saving our lives."

"You're welcome. It's my job. Don't like it when a job ends like this, but considering the circumstances, I couldn't see it resolving in any other way."

He has a point. I just wish for Tatum's sake, he would've left her the hell alone, so she didn't have to carry the burden or grief.

"I'll let you kids go. Make sure to call your damn brother," he barks out with a laugh, then walks away.

"Please tell me it's finally over," Tatum says, and I can see the exhaustion written on her face.

"It's over, baby," I confirm. Rubbing a hand down her arm, I lead her to the car. Once she's settled into the passenger's side and I climb behind the wheel, I call Tristan.

"Told ya so," he says as soon as he picks up.

I huff out a breath. "Guess I deserved that. But thank you for being a know-it-all, overbearing brother. You saved our lives."

"I wish I'd been wrong about my gut feeling, but I'm so damn relieved Bear was there."

"Where did you even find that guy? His nickname should be *Moose*. The man is huge!"

Piper giggles in the background, then responds, "Let's just say…a friend of a friend of a friend."

"I just knew that psychopath wasn't going to stop. All joking aside, I wouldn't be able to live with myself if something happened to you," Tristan says.

"How did you know, though? How did you anticipate Justin's actions?"

"Throughout the years, I've learned that some people can't let things go. A person capable of burning down someone's business to get back at their ex has loose screws, and no amount of mediation, agreeing, or pleading will make them stop. You were standing in the way of Tatum. So getting rid of you would've been a bonus in his eyes. Unfortunately for him, I couldn't let that happen."

"Me either!" Piper yells.

"Thank you. From both of us."

Tatum grabs my hand, and I kiss her knuckles. She's still in shock.

"So tell me what happened," he says. "I haven't talked to Bear yet. He just texted me *target deceased, clients safe.*"

"Jesus." I exhale. "Well…let me start from the beginning."

I explain our day, nearly minute to minute, and by the end, Tristan releases an annoyed groan.

"Easton, I want to chew your ass out right now and tell you everything you did wrong, but I know it won't do any good. So instead, I'll just say this—I'm glad you're both safe and alive. I love you guys."

"Love you too, bro."

I'm lucky my brother knows me so well and always looks out for me even when I don't think I need it.

"You have permission to relax now," he tells me with a soft laugh.

"I guess you can, too," I retort.

We say our goodbyes, but then Piper snatches the cell from my brother.

"So, have you proposed yet?" she blurts out without any sort of filter.

"Oh my God, Piper. You're on speakerphone!" I scold, but a smile touches Tatum's lips.

"Oh, whoops. Hi, Tatum! Don't mind me."

"It's fine," Tatum says, and I can tell she's out of it.

"Anyway, I think we need to make our way back to the house. We've had a long, exhausting day."

"No problem! Bye, you two lovebirds," Piper sing-songs, then she ends the call.

On the way home, Tatum closes her eyes and falls asleep. I hold her hand and softly rub the pad of my thumb over hers.

When I park in the driveway, I can see how mentally and physically exhausted she is.

"You okay?" I ask once we make it inside.

She shrugs, and I open my arms, allowing her to fall into them. I can smell the sweet scent of her coconut shampoo mixed with sweat.

"It's okay to be sad and upset. I know you loved him at one point, and everything happened so fast it's hard to comprehend it all. I can't imagine what's going through your mind right now."

I can tell she's crying, and all I want to do is hold her for the rest of the night. Once she's let most of it out, she pushes back and meets my eyes. I wipe away her tears.

"I don't know how I should feel about any of this."

"I'm sure it's hard to put into words. Whatever you're feeling is a hundred percent valid."

"Yeah. I feel guilty for being relieved. Like I'm finally free, and the shackles are gone. But I never wanted him dead."

"I know, sweetheart." I tuck a loose strand of hair behind her ear.

"He would've killed me, Easton. He wouldn't have stopped until I was dead."

I clear my throat, hating how much truth is behind those words. But after seeing the maniacal look on that man's face as he pointed his gun, I know she's right.

"There's no way I would've let that happen."

"Then you'd be dead. Either way, I lose. That's how the game was played with Justin. The cards were always stacked against me no matter what. He wouldn't have stopped. And I almost lost you. I saw him throw a blow at your head, then he pointed the gun at you." Then he aimed it at her. *Motherfucker*.

Her emotions boil over again, and I try to calm her down.

"Let it out, baby. I'm here with you. I always will be."

She cries for as long as she needs, and when she settles down, I pull away and meet her big blue eyes. "Do you want to take a bath? With me?" I ask, knowing it'd do us both good.

She nods and gives me a small grin. We go to the bathroom, and I draw the water while she lights candles. Carefully, I undress her and notice the marks on her arm. Tatum tries to pull away, but I don't let her. Instead, I kiss every single tiny bruise and scrape he left on her. "You'll never have to worry about this again."

I hate that he grabbed her while under my watch. Even more so that he laid his hands on her. If Bear hadn't gotten to him first, I would've done whatever it took to stop him.

She steps into the tub, and I follow her. As she leans against my chest, I wrap my arms around her. Tatum lets out a sigh and relaxes against me. We take our time washing up and stay snapped together like two puzzle pieces. When our skin has pruned, we get out and dry off, then go to my bedroom.

Lifting the sheets and blankets, I allow a naked Tatum to

crawl underneath. I join her, wrapping her tight in my arms, thanking my lucky stars we're alive.

Tatum rolls over and faces me. "Will you make love to me?"

I search her face, making sure I heard her correctly. "Of course," I whisper, then gently press my lips to hers. She devours my mouth as I brush my hand over her hard nipple, then down her stomach. Our tongues twist together, and I know I can't wait to be inside her much longer.

We take it slow as I move on top of her, holding myself up. She opens her legs wide, repositioning her body, giving me all the space I need to slide inside. Tatum gasps, slamming her eyes shut, allowing me to sink in all the way.

Right now, I don't want to rush. I want to enjoy every damn minute I have with this woman. She's changed my life for the better, and as long as she wants me, I'm hers. I've never felt this way about anyone before.

She digs her heels into my ass, encouraging me to go harder.

"Yes, yes, yes," she says, pulling me down to continue kissing her. Tatum's moans are like music to my ears, and I only wish she knew how much she means to me. After today, and knowing that it could've ended in tragedy, I know I can't wait to tell her.

"Harder," she groans, and I give her exactly what she wants. Her soft pants and warm breath against my skin drive me crazy. I kiss her again and again until both our lips are swollen.

"I'm so close," Tatum mumbles, her hair splashed across the pillow. "Come with me."

"Wait for me, baby," I say, feeling the build in the pit of my stomach.

Her back arches as I slam into her, and as soon as she

begins riding out her release, I lose myself inside her. The emotions stream through me, and I kiss Tatum until we're both gasping for air. I pet her damp hair and look into her eyes.

"I love you, Tatum," I say confidently, hoping she knows how much I mean it. "You don't have to say it back, but after what happened, I knew I couldn't go another day without telling you how much you mean to me."

"Easton, I love you too. I've known it for so long and was scared to open my heart to someone again, but I can't deny it. I love you so much."

We're smiling and kissing, and I've never quite felt happiness like this. It's everything. After we clean up, Tatum snuggles in my arms, and I hold her while staring up at the ceiling. I think the smile on my face might be permanent.

"There's something I wanted to ask you," I nervously say.

"Hmm," she responds, and I can tell she's falling asleep.

"Will you move in with me?"

Tatum turns her body so she can look into my eyes. "Really?"

"Yes, I can't imagine not holding you every night or waking up next to you. I'm addicted to this, Tatum. How could I sleep at night knowing the woman of my dreams is across the hall when she should be with me? I could have them remodel the entire upstairs area into one big condo so we'll have a bigger joint space. Then we can run the shop together too, as equal partners."

"Are you sure about all that?" She searches my face. "That's a huge commitment, Easton. You've spent your time and money on that shop. You've put everything into it."

"And I want to share that with you, my love. I've been thinking about this, and I've never been more sure about anything in my life. I know you're the woman for me, Tatum. But I also don't want you to feel pressured or rushed to do anything. Moving in together would be a first big step, a leap that I'm willing to take, but only if you want it. If you don't, I won't be ups—"

Tatum presses her lips against mine to stop me from rambling. "Yes," she says, beaming. "Yes, Easton. I'd love that so much. You have no idea how happy you've made me."

I pull her into my arms and kiss her softly, almost like we're in a dream I don't want to wake from. "You're so damn beautiful," I tell her as she straddles me.

"And I'm yours," Tatum says, sliding onto my cock. She rocks her hips, this time taking complete control.

We make love again until our bodies can't take anymore, then fall asleep tangled together. I'm in love with an intelligent, thoughtful woman, who's given her heart to me when she hardly had any to offer, and it feels so good to tell her as much.

CHAPTER TWENTY

TATUM

TWO MONTHS LATER

ROLLING OVER, I see the sun splashing across the hardwood floor of our condo. The renovations were finally complete a couple weeks ago and we moved right in. It's even better than I expected and am so happy living with Easton, I could burst. It's been two months since Justin attacked us and we've been inseparable ever since.

We did have to go to court to testify about how we'd been stalked. Thankfully, Bear had enough evidence to make the case clear cut. It was ruled as self-defense because of Justin's unlawful aggression, plus the fact he had kidnapped me at gunpoint after a warrant was issued for his arrest. To say I was relieved when it was all put to rest is an understatement.

Easton's arm snakes around me, and he pulls me against his morning wood. I rub my ass against him and let out a hum.

"I will never get tired of having your warm body next to me like this," he says into my ear, his chin hair tickling my neck. Moments later, Easton's alarm on his phone goes off, and he rolls over to turn it off.

"I can't believe it's already seven," he says, coming back to me.

I meet his face. "Are you excited about today?"

"Yes. A little nervous, though. It's been a while," he explains. Today is the grand re-opening of the shop. While we missed the summer rush, the locals are excited to support Easton, especially since the shop had a complete remodel.

"It's just like riding a bike," I tell him.

"As long as you're with me, that's all that matters," he says before sliding his lips across mine. Seconds later, I'm slipping my panties off and climbing on top of him.

"Damn, baby. I love how you wake up ready," he tells me, digging his thumbs into my hips as I slide down his cock.

When he's entirely inside me, I lean down and whisper in his ear. "Best part of waking up is having your cock inside me. I can't get enough of you."

He grabs a handful of my ass. "I hope you never do."

After I ride him for a few minutes, he flips me onto all fours, then scoots me to the edge of the bed. My ass is in the air as he slowly guides himself into me from behind.

"More," I moan, grasping fistfuls of the comforter.

Easton slams into me hard, the way I like. When he reaches around to flick my clit with his fingers, my body is ready to collapse.

"You're so goddamn wet, baby," he says, our skin slapping together each time he slams inside me.

"You do that to me," I moan. Seconds later, Easton slaps my ass cheeks. The pain mixes with pleasure, and it causes my pussy to throb with excitement.

"You drive me fucking crazy," Easton states, his movements

slowing and becoming more calculated. At any minute, we'll both fall over the edge.

While I'm teetering on edge, he pulls out, drops to his knees, then devours me from behind. His tongue moves between my clit and my pussy, and the sensation is so intense the orgasm nearly blinds me.

As I'm coming, he slides back inside me and fucks me so good. I reach back and massage his balls, and seconds later, he's releasing inside me. I buck beneath him, creating as much friction as I can. After we quickly clean up, we both lie back on the bed and stare at the ceiling, trying to catch our breaths.

He turns to me and smiles before pressing his soft lips against mine. "I love you, Tatum."

"I love you more," I say, and he reaches over to try to tickle me.

"No!" I try to push him away, but he's too fast and strong. "You're going to make me pee myself!" I screech, standing and running to the bathroom.

"I'm gonna get you for that!" I tell him, and he stands at the doorway and watches me.

"Let's take a shower," he suggests, turning on the water, and when I'm done doing my business, I join him.

Easton washes every inch of my body, massaging my scalp with shampoo and even conditioning my hair too. He brushes his lips softly against my neck, and when it's his turn, I take pride in lathering his cock.

"God," he moans out, pressing his palm against the shower wall. "Do you have any idea how many times I've jacked off to this image before we got together?"

I drop down to my knees, then take him in my mouth, meeting his eyes. "Tell me," I say, making sure to lick his sensitive tip.

"At least a hundred. I used to fantasize about you even though I knew it was wrong since I was your boss."

I take him to the back of my throat, wanting to choke on his length and girth.

"What did you want to do?" I ask, stroking him before bringing him back to my lips.

"Devour your pussy. Watch you swallow my come. One time, you were wearing a shirt, and I could see your perky little nipples, and I imagined sucking on them."

"Mmm," I purr, picking up my pace, wanting to taste him this time.

"Tatum," he groans, fisting my wet hair as I hold his thighs. I meet his eyes, and when his muscles flex, I brace myself. I shove him in and out of my mouth as he empties himself down my throat. When I've swallowed every drop, I stand and lick my lips.

"You're so fucking sexy," he says, crashing his lips against mine.

I smirk. "You are too."

I finish washing him then we get out and dry off. We quickly have breakfast, then get dressed. It's evident that Easton is nervous about today, and I try to calm his nerves. It's a big deal, and many of the other businesses in the area are having sidewalk sales to draw more customers to the area. Piper has also gotten several influencers together to come out and celebrate. The local news stations will be interviewing Easton about what happened to give the shop more exposure. So, I understand why he feels this way.

Before we go downstairs to open the shop, he pulls me into his arms. "Thank you for being here with me."

"There is honestly nowhere else on this planet I'd rather be right now. Today is going to run flawlessly, and we're going to sell a lot of new items."

"I hope you're right," he says.

"It's called manifesting," I quip. "Oakley is a queen at it."

"I love it," he says, kissing me before we head downstairs.

As soon as he turns on the lights, a few employees scheduled for today begin to trickle in. Pop music plays overhead, and I look around, amazed by how updated the place is. The LED lights and huge windows in the front really brighten up the place. Easton purchased a bunch of old surfboards to display, and it's hard not to love the new vibe. We even got an updated computer system to make checking people out easier. The layout will help him sell more than before, and I can't wait to see how it goes.

Soon, Easton unlocks the door, and to my surprise, a line of people stands outside waiting to enter. Within five minutes, the shop is packed so full that I'm scared the fire marshall will shut the place down.

The influencers Piper scheduled arrive, and then the next thing I know, it's a madhouse. Easton walks around and helps people find items while I stay at the counter with Nova and ring people up. It's nonstop scanning and swiping debit cards. Aubree stays busy restocking items as soon as the shelves go bare, and though hours pass, it feels like a few minutes.

The news station arrives, and Easton is pulled outside in front of the shop. He makes eye contact with me and waves me over. When a new hire named Jalinda steps in, I join him. I'm amazed the sidewalk is still full of people waiting to enter.

Easton smiles and pulls me close as the news anchor and cameraman count down.

"Here we are with Easton Belvedere, the twenty-eight-year-old who owns Belvedere's Surf and Suits. A tragedy ensued a few months ago, and his shop burned to the ground. Today is the grand re-opening. Easton, please tell us a little bit about your shop."

Looking like a movie star, Easton wraps his arm around me and explains his love for the sport and why he decided to make a business out of his passion.

"That's incredible," she states.

"It really is. If it weren't for my girlfriend, who encouraged me to keep going and helped make sure we opened in a timely manner, I'm not sure we'd be standing here right now."

I smile at the camera, heat meeting my cheeks. "Please don't let him downplay it. He's so passionate about surfing that this would've happened without me. I'm just honored that I've been able to help in the ways that I can."

"So, Tatum, what do you love most about the shop?"

I laugh. "That's easy. It makes a huge difference when you have someone running a place like this who actually loves surfing. Easton is an honest and kind man willing to help people when they're lost. Without him in the forefront, there would be no shop. I think it's one of the strengths of the business and why I think it will be around for decades to come."

"That's incredible. Anything else you'd like to add to that, Easton?" She holds the microphone out for him.

"We'll be here until six today, and you can find out our store hours on the website. You can always shop online if you don't feel like getting out. Don't forget to use the hashtag Belvedere Surf to all of your beach posts to be entered to win a five-hundred-dollar gift certificate. No purchase necessary!"

"You heard it from the owner, folks. Come out and see them, buy some suits or accessories, and don't forget about that giveaway."

The cameraman counts down, and as soon as we're off the air, they both thank us. Immediately, Easton leans over and kisses me. "You're too good to me."

I grab the bottom hem of his shirt. "You can prove it to me later tonight."

"Deal." He bites my bottom lip between his teeth.

"Ahem." I hear from behind us, and when Easton turns, he laughs.

"Tristan," he states, his brother pulling him into a hug.

"You know I couldn't miss this," he says with Piper close to him, who's wearing oversized sunglasses that cover her face and a baggy T-shirt to hide her bump.

"Oh my God! Tatum!" she yelps and pulls me into a hug. Of course, paparazzi take photos from across the street, but it's all for exposure. "Finally, I get to meet you! And you're gorgeous."

"I owe you triple hugs for everything you've done for us!" I explain, squeezing her again. "Look at how adorable you are."

I glance down at her pregnant belly, and she places a hand on it. "Thank you. Still trying to get used to it all."

"I'm sure you'll adjust just fine," I offer.

"We should probably go inside," Tristan says, escorting Piper inside. Easton places his arm on my shoulder.

"Aren't you glad I'm not your crazy protective bodyguard?" he whispers in my ear.

"Oh, you aren't?" I turn and meet his eyes as we go to the stockroom. Several employees go in and out from the back, grabbing more items.

"I didn't expect you two to show up!" Easton says, hugging Piper.

"Are you surprised?" she asks.

"Of course, I am," he tells her. "It's been so long."

"Good! Tonight, I have something really special planned for us after you close. I mean, if you're available. Don't feel obligated if you have plans."

Easton turns to me, and I smile. "We'd love to join you."

"We need some more change," Nova says.

"We better let you two get back to it. You've got a store full of customers to take care of," Tristan says. "We're probably going to go out the back. Check out the beach house, then meet you back here."

"Sounds good," Easton tells me. We say our goodbyes, then immediately go out to the front. Easton and I run around like chickens with our heads cut off, and when the last customer of the day finally leaves, we're ready to collapse.

"That was worse than Black Friday," Aubree says.

"It was." Easton clears his throat. "Just want to tell you all thank you so much for working today. I've decided to pay you all time and a half. The schedule has been posted for the rest of the week, and if we keep this up, I'll probably look at hiring a few more people, so let your friends know. Now, let's clean this place up and get out of here."

They let out hoots and hollers, then we work as a team to clean up and restock. Easton counts the money in the drawers, and when he's done, shock is written all over his face.

I lean across the counter and tap next to the register with my hand. "Everything okay?"

"We sold over a hundred thousand dollars' worth of items," he mutters. "How is this possible?"

A laugh escapes me. "I believe it. The place was packed for eight hours straight with a constant line outside."

"I'm a little overwhelmed by this," he admits.

I move around the counter. "Did you recount to make sure?"

"I triple counted. It's right. Damn." A wide grin slides across Easton's lips, and I hold up my hand. He gives me a high five and lets out a woot.

"Seriously, that's a record."

I stand on my tiptoes and kiss him. "You deserve it, love."

"We do," he tells me.

After everyone leaves and the place is locked up, we go upstairs. Easton and I both fall back on the couch, my feet killing me from standing for so long. Thirty minutes later, Piper and Easton arrive.

"The beach house looks so good," Piper says, sitting right next to me on the couch. "How'd today go?"

Easton tells her how much money he dropped off to deposit, and Tristan is shocked. Piper gives him a knowing nod.

"I won the bet," she tells Tristan. "You're paying up."

"That's not fair. You made sure people would show up. We bet before you had your friends come and greet people." Tristan groans.

"A bet is a bet," Piper says with a devilish smirk.

"Wait, you two bet on how much I'd make?" Easton asks.

"Yes, and just know who was on your side," Piper tells him. "Me. I said you'd make over six figures, and Tristan said you wouldn't."

"I'm glad you lost," he tells his brother, and we all burst into laughter.

"I deserve that," Tristan says. "I'm glad it all worked out for the best."

"So, what did you guys have in mind for tonight?" Easton asks, looking between Piper and Tristan.

"It's a surprise," Piper tells us, then looks down at her phone. "Are we ready?"

"Yes." I stand, overly excited about what we're going to do tonight.

We make our way downstairs and see a limo waiting for us on the street. As soon as we climb in, Tristan pours us all a glass of champagne, except for Piper. Then Piper pulls out the chocolate-covered strawberries and takes one.

"So good," she says, snatching another one. We make small talk for about thirty minutes until we pull into the airport.

"Wait, where are we going?" Easton asks once he realizes where we are.

"I said it was a surprise! Don't try to ruin it now!" Piper playfully scolds. "You'll be back in time to open the shop in the morning."

Tristan chuckles as I wait with anticipation and notice a helicopter sitting on a pad.

"Whoa," I whisper. "Are we getting on that?"

"Yes, yes, we are," Piper states. "I can't wait to see Florida from above."

The limo comes to a stop, and the driver opens our door. We're escorted onto the helicopter that's got comfortable leather seats. Each of us is given a headset so we can still chat with one another while we're in the air.

Easton sits right next to me and interlocks his fingers with mine. He leans close, moving the headphone from my ear, and whispers, "I love you."

I mouth it back to him.

"This is my favorite part," Piper says as we hover over the ground, then take off. We fly over the coast, and I love seeing the sunset from above. It's beautiful, and I can't stop staring.

"I've never been in a helicopter before," Easton says, and I agree.

Tristan is holding Piper as they look out the window. "You get used to it," he tells us.

Eventually, the helicopter flies over the beach, and torches are lit that say congrats. It slowly descends and stops on a pad.

"Where are we?" Easton asks as we step out.

"On a private beach," Piper explains, leading us to an

overwater bungalow. As we get closer to the deck, I see a string quartet, a private chef and server, and several different wines. I can't even imagine how much this cost.

"Piper," I whisper.

"Before you say anything, this is my personal treat. I just wanted us to have privacy without all the attention." She squeezes me. "Plus, look at this view."

Turning, I see the golden rays of the evening sunset bursting over the water. Orange and pink fill the sky as a warm breeze brushes over my skin. I inhale slowly, taking in the moment. Easton's eyes meet mine, and he grabs my hand to kiss my knuckles.

We sit at the table as the music drifts in the background. There's laughter and love, and Easton randomly leans in and kisses me every chance he gets. The chef allows us to order and prepares our food in the outdoor kitchen.

The salmon and shrimp are fresh, along with the veggies. Everything tastes so damn good that I have to hold back moans each time I take a bite. At the end of the meal, we're served the chocolate cake with homemade ice cream. As I look around the table, I'm so happy that I nearly tear up.

"I don't know what I did in my past life to deserve any of this, but thank you all so much," I say, trying to hold my emotions in.

Easton wraps his arm around me. "You deserve the world, beautiful."

"You're basically family now," Tristan tells me, and Piper nods in agreement. It's so cute how they look at each other with so much love and adoration, and I know Easton gives me the same look.

"Sometimes, bad things happen, which leads you to the person you're supposed to be with," Piper says. "I just knew this was going to happen when I was told you'd be staying at the beach house together. I like to think that I helped with the matchmaking."

Easton chuckles. "Oh, hush. I fell in love with Tatum the moment I saw her. The beach house just allowed us to get to know each other better. But yeah, I agree, wouldn't change it for the world because it all worked out in the end."

I think about everything I've been through over the years. All the heartache, tragedy, and loss made me realize I found happiness by following my heart. Little did I know I'd find the man of my dreams in Florida. Every day I wake up, I feel so damn thankful I left because everything worked out the way it was supposed to.

CHAPTER TWENTY-ONE

EASTON

ONE MONTH LATER

IT'S BEEN three months since Justin attacked us and now we're both ready for a break from how busy the shop has been these past few weeks. Since Oakley couldn't come out for the re-opening, I decided to surprise Tatum with a trip to see her. I didn't tell her until we got to airport security.

As soon as she saw CALIFORNIA on the tickets, she immediately knew. The flight was fine, but now we're waiting for an Uber to take us to our hotel.

"I can't believe we're here and gonna surf!" she gushes, wrapping her arms around my neck.

"Well, you can't go to the West Coast and *not* surf. That'd be a crime."

"Have you ever visited before?" she asks.

"Nope. This is a first for me too." I kiss the tip of her nose.

Once we check in to the Radisson, we crash for a short nap. Then we have plans to meet Oakley for dinner at a Mexican restaurant.

"Oh my gosh!" Tatum squeals as soon as she sees her. The

moment is like a slow-motion scene in a rom-com where long-lost siblings run into each other's arms.

"Holy crap, I can't believe you're both standing in front of me." Oakley's smile matches Tatum's.

I stand once they separate. "Finally, meeting the famous little sister."

"In the flesh." She hugs me. "Though, famous...? Not yet anyway. Maybe someday." She waggles her brows.

Tatum showed me some of Oakley's paintings, and I agree, her work is incredible. There's no doubt she has a bright future ahead of her.

We sit, then place our drink and food orders.

"Catch me up with school," Tatum says.

"It's going pretty well. I hit a creative block a few months ago, but it's starting to come back. I have one year of grad classes left, so no getting married before then."

"Oakley!" Tatum hisses, kicking her underneath the table.

"I'm just saying! I want to help plan and stuff since I'll obviously be your maid of honor, but it'd be best for my schedule if you waited until after I graduated. Just in case anyone was wondering."

I hold back my thoughts as I drink my beer and think about how much I want Tatum to be my wife. There's no doubt that she's the one. Not only have we gone through a lot in a short amount of time, but I'm fucking crazy about her and can't imagine life without her.

"Sucks I can't meet you two for surfing tomorrow morning," Oakley says.

Tatum snorts, dipping a chip in salsa. "Yeah, I'm sure you are."

"Sorry I didn't have a personal tutor." Oakley shoots her gaze to me with a smirk. "I'd probably be a pro, too, if I had."

"I'm not a pro," Tatum counters.

"Not *yet*. Pretty close, though." I flash her a wink.

She shakes her head. "I'm only doing it for fun, nothing else," she confirms.

We stick around the restaurant for two hours, drinking, eating, and catching up. The longer I listen to them, the more similarities I see. Even though they're different in almost every way, their personalities and mannerisms resemble each other.

"Okay, so we'll see each other again after your classes tomorrow night?" Tatum confirms as they hug goodbye.

"Yep, should be ready by five. I'm going to take you guys to the most amazing hibachi. Just don't get too close, or it'll burn your eyebrows off."

We chuckle and say goodbye, then Tatum and I take an Uber back to the hotel.

"I love California so far," Tatum says as we walk hand in hand down the sidewalk.

I chuckle because we've been here less than twelve hours.

"Maybe it needs a Belvedere Surf Shop right on the boardwalk."

"You trying to find ways to get rid of me already?"

She squeezes my fingers. "Nope, never. It was just a thought. I haven't traveled much, obviously, so any new place you take me, I'll probably want to stay."

"Remind me to never take you to New York. The moment you see Tristan and Piper's penthouse, you'd never want to leave."

She bursts out laughing. "I'm not that level of high maintenance."

"Oh really? Do I need to bring up the cabinet's debate again?" I arch a brow, and she immediately rolls her eyes.

"Shush your mouth, or you aren't getting laid tonight."

A person walking in the other direction gives her the side-eye, and I beam at the way Tatum shrugs it off. She no longer gets easily embarrassed or cares who overhears her. She's found her self-confidence, and I love seeing her this way. Not only is she much happier than before, but so am I.

The following morning, we're up by six to rent our boards. We brought our surfing gear, and once we had everything we needed, we walked to the beach.

"I'm so excited!" she gushes as we walk through the sand barefoot.

"Me too, babe. Gonna be so fun." It's just after seven when the sun starts to rise. Some others are here already, but we manage to find a decent spot.

"Wow, it's beautiful." Tatum beams at the view, and I wrap my arms around her waist from behind.

"You sure are," I murmur.

She snickers, but I'll never stop telling her that.

"Well, you ready to get in?"

"Yes! Oh my God, it's gonna be so cold."

"Let's get it over with," I suggest.

We stick our boards in the sand and race in. As soon as my knees collide with the water, I dive in.

"That'll wake you right up," I say, slicking back my wet hair.

"More than coffee," Tatum adds with a laugh.

We grab our boards and attach our ankle straps, then head in. Once we're waist-deep, we paddle a little farther out, then sit on top. As we float and wait for the perfect swell, I turn to her. She's about twenty feet away from me, but I speak loud so she can hear me.

"So I was thinking about what Oakley said last night."

She furrows her brows. "About what?"

"Us getting married," I remind her, looking in the distance at a swell building. Tatum's gotten so good she can catch the wave before it fully breaks and stay steady through the white water.

"Ignore her, seriously. She speaks before she thinks."

"So you don't want to?"

"What?"

I lick my lips and grin. "Get married!" I shout.

"You wanna get *married*?"

On cue, we position ourselves in the middle of our boards, then start paddling.

"I wanna marry *you*," I confirm as the wave catches us.

"Are you being serious?"

Just as she practiced all those months ago, Tatum pops up, and I follow her lead. We're soaring across the liquid glass, and I watch her stance as she takes complete control of the board. The water rolls as she leads the board right before the break, then zooms across the white water like she's been surfing for at least five years.

"Whew, that was a good one!" I shout, catching up to her.

When we're both on the sand, Tatum turns toward me. "Easton, you can't just mention getting married and then paddle away!"

I chuckle at how flustered she sounds.

"I couldn't help it! You know it was a good one," I defend, then change my tone. "So?"

"So what?"

"I'm still waiting for your answer."

She blinks at me, frazzled. "Are you asking me to marry you, or are you asking if I want to get married?"

"I'm asking you to marry me."

"See, I can't tell if you're kidding or not."

I take her shaky hands in mine. "I'm dead serious. Will you make George the happiest hamster alive and marry his daddy?"

Her hand flies to her mouth as a combination of laughter and sobs surface. "You're really serious!"

Finally, I get down on one knee to prove that I'm not joking. "Tatum, you once told me that when the right person comes along, I'd know. You said waiting to find *the one* was worth it. And I've waited years for you, so you'd be crazy to think I'm ever letting you go. I know in my heart that you're it for me and that we're meant for each other, but if you're not ready for this step, that's okay too. Someday I'm making you my wife."

She nods, wiping tears off her cheeks, and finally whispers, "Yes."

"Yes?" I ask, making sure I heard her correctly.

"Yes! *Yes*, I'll marry you!" She giggles as I stand and lift her in my arms.

"It's about damn time!"

"We've been together for literally four months," she reminds me when I set her down.

"And I was ready to marry you after one." I shoot her a wink.

She playfully rolls her eyes. "You're crazy."

"Crazy about you." I grab her hand and kiss her knuckles. "We can go pick out a ring together. That way, you can choose the one you like."

"You didn't plan this?"

"Not exactly, but I've wanted to ask you since we moved into the condo. I couldn't imagine waking up without you beside me. When Oakley brought it up, I knew the time was now."

"She's going to gloat like hell. You know that, right?"

I shrug. "That's what younger siblings do. Just have to make sure we plan it a year out, so she doesn't lose her shit."

She laughs. "Too bad. I don't think I can wait a year."

My brows shoot up. "Is that so, future Mrs. Belvedere?" I pull her into my arms.

"Yeah, I like the sound of that way too much." She smirks. "Let's have a spring wedding."

"Deal." I tilt up her chin and kiss her mouth. "My promise to you is to give you whatever you want and need, baby. You're my heart and soul."

"I love you," she whispers.

"I love you more."

The next three days in California fly by. Oakley freaked out as soon as we gave her the news. Then we spent an entire day ring shopping and another with Oakley trying to convince us to get married in Hawaii. After thinking about it, we decided it wasn't a bad idea after all. Plus, the surfing in Hawaii is incredible.

Before we came to the airport this morning, Oakley stopped by our hotel to say one more final goodbye. The girls cried, and I promised to let her stay at the beach house some time. As sad as we were to leave, we were ready to share the news with everyone.

We FaceTimed my brother and Piper that same day. They both were so excited. Piper's already giving me a mile-long wedding to-do list and insisted on letting her hire a wedding planner.

I declined her offer, but of course, she wouldn't shut up about it until Tatum finally gave in. With the stipulation that she doesn't go overboard. We all know that's going to happen anyway.

As Tatum and I finally board our flight to Florida, I whisper in her ear, "Want to have another first together and cross one more place off the sex bucket list?"

She smirks at the idea of joining the mile-high club. "Let's do it, future hubby."

EPILOGUE
TATUM

ONE YEAR LATER

I've waited for what feels like an eternity for this day, and it being here is giving me major anxiety.

After Easton and I got married in Hawaii five months ago, we started the process of finding a surrogate. It's something we started talking about after we got engaged. Although I have PTSD from losing my son eleven years ago, I'm finally ready to try again. Since I'm thirty-eight and have never had a healthy pregnancy, the risks were too high to try to conceive. Of course, if it happened, it happened, but it was safer for my mental and physical health that it didn't.

Our surrogate, Kyrie, has her ultrasound today, and we'll find out if we're having a boy or a girl. We met her through a company Piper recommended, and she swore they were the best of the best. Four months ago, Kyrie got a positive test, and we've been staying in contact with her ever since.

Kyrie lives in the Midwest, so we can't be there for her appointment today, but her husband is FaceTiming us during the scan. I've been pacing for thirty minutes, awaiting their call.

"Tatum, you're going to wear a hole in the carpet if you don't sit," Easton calmly tells me.

"I can't help it," I say, plopping down on the couch and shaking my knee. I'm beyond excited but also nervous. At twenty weeks, they can get a better view of the baby to get measurements and make sure he or she is healthy.

"Piper's blowing up my phone. She's dying to find out."

She and I both.

Tristan and Piper had two baby girls, named Della and Delilah, seven months ago. Now she's eager for us to have a girl too so that all three can be best friend cousins.

My phone vibrates on the table, and I leap to grab it. I click on the screen and am greeted by Kyrie's sweet smile. "Hey, we're here," she says quietly.

Easton sits next to me and waves. We chat for a few minutes until the radiologist finishes setting up. Then her husband takes the phone and points us to the monitor.

The woman performing the exam talks us through everything she's doing and what she's measuring. I nearly burst into tears when I see tiny hands and a button nose.

"The baby has your features," Kyrie tells me, and I smile.

"Are we ready to find out the gender?" the woman asks in an excited voice.

"Yes!" we all exclaim.

"Alright, let's see if they'll cooperate."

The seconds that pass while she searches seem like the longest ones of my life. Finally, she captures a picture and freezes it on the screen.

"It's a girl!"

"Oh my God!" I would've been happy with either but knowing for sure is just so exciting.

"Congrats, Mom and Dad," the woman says.

"Now to come up with a name," I ponder, and Kyrie chuckles. She knows Easton and I haven't agreed on one yet.

After they're done, she tells me she'll call me later, and we hang up.

"It feels so real now," I whisper when Easton captures my lips.

"We're gonna have a daughter," he says with a grin. "She's probably going to wrap me around her little finger too."

"Oh, one-thousand percent." I chuckle.

"Well, who should we tell first?" he asks.

"Piper," I say. She'll blow a blood vessel if we make her wait any longer.

"Hey!" she squeals as soon as her face appears on the screen. She's holding the twins in her lap, who are dressed up like they're going to a ball. They each have big bows in their hair and are wearing equally big dresses. "Did you find out?"

"Girl!" I blurt it out. "We're having a girl."

"Ahh! Did you hear that, girls?" She bounces them on her legs. "I'm so excited!"

"Congrats, guys." Tristan walks in from behind. "Your life is about to be turned upside down with pink bows and poopy diapers."

We chuckle.

"Probably not as much as yours was," Easton counters.

"Sounds perfect to me," I say as I gaze at my husband.

A life with him has been better than I could've ever imagined. Having a baby girl and starting a family with the man I love feels too good to be true.

EASTON

Even though Tatum didn't want to try to get pregnant again, she's been glowing since the moment we found out the surrogacy worked. I knew I wanted to start a family with her, and if this option had failed, we would've tried another. Though adoption is something we're still considering in the future.

"Ready to call my obnoxious sister?" Tatum asks.

I chuckle. "Sure."

Oakley picks up after one ring, and by the look on her face, she's aggravated.

"Hey," she says, and her mood shifts. "Do we have the news?"

"Let me tell her," I say before Tatum can. She furrows her brows at me. "You told Piper!"

"But Oakley's my sister! I wanna tell her."

"How come I didn't get to tell my brother then?" I counter.

"Oh my God!" Oakley snaps. "Will one of you just freaking tell me? Is it a taco or a frank and beans?"

"Ew!" Tatum scowls. "Don't be inappropriate about your niece."

I gasp in shock. "You little cheater!"

Tatum giggles, pushing me away when I try to tackle her.

"Yay, it's a girl! Now, let's discuss my niece's name."

"You're not picking it," I blurt out.

"Oh, come on. I'm not having kids for like thirty years. Let me choose."

"Then get a puppy, and you can name it whatever you want," I say firmly. Knowing Oakley, she'll want some flowery hippie name like *Blossom* or *Freesia*.

"You owe me, *brother-in-law*." She emphasizes each word.

"How so?" I cross my arms over my chest.

"If it weren't for me, you would've never asked my sister to marry you that day. You probably wouldn't even be engaged right now."

"Nah, that's not true," I state, but she has a point. Her conversation sparked the idea to propose at the beach.

"It's kinda true..." Tatum interjects. "I mean, we would've gotten engaged eventually, I'm sure."

I sigh. "Fine, I will agree to this on *one* condition."

"Okay, what is it?"

Before I can respond, a door slams behind Oakley, and she groans loudly. "Great, he's back."

"Uh, who?"

"Finn," she says with disdain. "The innkeeper's grandson whose only life goal is to make mine miserable."

Tatum breaks out in a smile. "The one you're staying with while you're there?"

"Yep," she hisses between her teeth, then leans in closer to the screen. "Please come rescue me."

Her pathetic tone has us suppressing our laughter. Oakley was commissioned to do some paintings for a vast family farm for its one-hundredth-year celebration. They flew her out to Vermont and asked that she get to know the land and all that it has to offer so she could fully represent its spirit in her work. Getting hired was a major deal and could bring in future jobs. She and Tatum talked about it at length for weeks.

"Oh my God." She rolls her eyes. "He just tossed his boots in the middle of the living room, then flung his shirt on the back of the couch. Oh, now he's digging through the fridge like a strung-out raccoon. Christ, they're raising Barbarians out here!"

This time, we can't hold back from laughing. It's her first time living out in the *real world*, and so far, it sounds like it hasn't been so kind to her.

"Just...give him a chance," Tatum tries to sound supportive. "They're culturally different up there."

Her lame reasoning has me furrowing my brows. She glares as if to tell me to keep my lips shut.

"It's not just that he's a slob, he's a jerk and all-around rude host. He brought a pizza in last night and ate the entire thing! Didn't even offer me *one* slice."

"Did you ask for one?" I inquire.

"No, but I shouldn't have to. It's called *manners*. Clearly, something he doesn't have," she scathes.

"I'm gonna take a bath. Maybe you should too. Try to relax," Tatum suggests.

"I'm not soaking in that tub. It probably hasn't been cleaned since the day it was built, which was a hundred years ago. How could anyone forget?" she sarcastically adds.

"Then take a walk to blow off some steam," I chime in.

She exhales slowly. "Shoving my fist in his mouth would help with that."

"Okay, well, don't do that. This is a great job opportunity, so don't mess it up just because you want to bang the asshole who won't give you the time of day."

Her jaw drops. "That is *so* not true. He'd probably give me rabies."

"*Oakley Jane*! Be nice."

"Fine." She rolls her eyes.

"Bye, sis," I sing-song.

"Wait, don't think I forgot about our agreement! Magnolia Rayne has an adorable ring to it, don't ya think?"

"Oh hell no. We're not naming our child after a flower." I turn to Tatum for backup, but she's pretending she doesn't see me. "Babe?"

She finally faces me and chews her bottom lip. "I kinda like it."

"Yes! I win!" Oakley cheers.

"We'll talk later," Tatum tells her, then quickly says goodbye.

"You can't be serious."

Tatum shrugs innocently. "We could call her Maggie."

I pinch the bridge of my nose, knowing I'll give in to whatever Tatum wants. "Alright, if that's what you really want, then I'm in."

"Seriously! You're the most amazing husband ever." She jumps into my lap and crashes her mouth to mine.

"Whatever we name her won't change how precious and amazing she'll be. She's going to be the perfect mixture of you and me."

"Yeah," she agrees. "The heart of us."

Curious about what happens with Finn and Oakley? Find out next in *The Fall of Us*

If you didn't start from the beginning, find Eli & Cami's story in The Two of Us, Ryan & Kendall's story in The Best of Us, and Tristan & Piper's story in The End of Us.

WHAT'S NEXT

Next in the Love in Isolation series is Finn & Oakley's story in *The Fall of Us*

What happens when you travel across the country for your dream job and end up having to stay with an older man who mocks your profession and makes crude comments? You show him who's in control and hope you don't fall in his trap—or his bed.

The Fall of us is an enemies to lovers, close proximity romance.

ABOUT THE AUTHOR

Brooke Cumberland and Lyra Parish are a duo of romance authors who teamed up under the *USA Today* pseudonym, Kennedy Fox. They share a love of Hallmark movies, overpriced coffee, and making TikToks. When they aren't bonding over romantic comedies, they like to brainstorm new book ideas. One day in 2016, they decided to collaborate under a pseudonym and have some fun creating new characters that'll make you blush and your heart melt. Happily ever afters guaranteed!

CONNECT WITH US

BOOKS BY KENNEDY FOX

DUET SERIES (BEST READ IN ORDER)

CHECKMATE DUET SERIES

ROOMMATE DUET SERIES

LAWTON RIDGE DUET SERIES

INTERCONNECTED STAND-ALONES

MAKE ME SERIES

BISHOP BROTHERS SERIES

CIRCLE B RANCH SERIES

LOVE IN ISOLATION SERIES

Find the entire Kennedy Fox reading order at
Kennedyfoxbooks.com/reading-order

Find all of our current freebies at
Kennedyfoxbooks.com/freeromance

CPSIA information can be obtained
at www.ICGtesting.com
Printed in the USA
LVHW031236020322
712194LV00007B/323